MOSQUITO COAST

GUILLAUME BONN

MOSQUITO COAST

Travels from Maputo to Mogadishu

Foreword by Jon Lee Anderson

HATJE
CANTZ

For many years I have been trying to come to terms with the changes that are transforming Africa into a place that is far removed from the familiar, comfortable Africa I knew as a child. Places that seemed frozen in time; places that reminded me of the colonial-era houses I had once lived in with my parents.

I am the third generation of a family of Frenchmen born in Madagascar. My father and grandfather spent their formative years on the island. My first memories are of Djibouti, an old French colonial outpost stuck between the Danakil Desert and the Indian Ocean. In my childhood, in the seventies, it was still part of France.

I grew up on the adventures of Henry de Monfreid, who built his fortune smuggling drugs and arms in his Arab dhow, eluding arrest by the French colonial authorities in Djibouti and by the English Navy based across the straits in Aden, Yemen. In Kenya, I met the famous explorer Wilfred Thesiger, the first white man to be born in Ethiopia, at the start of the twentieth century. He had crossed Arabia's Empty Quarter by foot several times, hunted lions in Sudan, and lived amongst the Marsh Arabs in Iraq. He was then an old man living a very simple life in a very remote and isolated area in northern Kenya. Meeting Thesiger was what put me on the path of wanting to "explore" Africa for myself.

In time I became a documentary photographer. I lived in Nairobi and traveled to every corner of the continent, witnessing and recording the continent's changes as they took place. Along the way, my own particular sense of Africa emerged as well, an alchemical mixture made up of the familiar—its fading European colonial heritage, architecture, and enduring lifestyles—together with the continent's devastating wars, its dictatorships, and the epic destruction of its natural environment, including its wildlife. I wished to somehow capture all of this visually. The idea persisted. For a long time, I could not imagine how to embark on such a project. I felt challenged by a number of seemingly unanswerable questions. How could I tell the story of my own memories of a world that no longer existed, or if it did, barely survived? How could I come to terms with my own family's role in the colonial brutality that the continent had experienced for a hundred years? How to avoid falling into the trap of all the romantic clichés of colonial Africa?

I have been trying for a long time to come to terms with the changes that are transforming Africa. We are told that progress is a good thing, that mobile phones and the Internet will make us all happier and our lives better. Along with those things, skyscrapers, highways, parking lots, and all the other accoutrements of consumerism have begun to find their way into Africa, and to change it, sometimes disastrously.

I have seen remote communities where the wholesale imposition of Western culture was eroding traditional, more sustainable ways of life.

It is strange and difficult for me to see the continent that I love, and that has made me and defined me, metamorphose so drastically.

I still catch glimpses of the past, but my feelings of nostalgia are painful. I cannot push away the sadness I have in me witnessing the transformation that is taking place in Africa before my eyes.

I decided that I needed to go back to where it all began, to the East African coastline, where, over the centuries, newcomers had arrived continuously from distant lands by boat, each bringing new influences with them and together creating the Africa I had grown up with. They came in waves, in trickles, and in different shapes and hues. There were conquerors, explorers, traders, and immigrants, and they included Portuguese, Omanis, Indians, British, Italians, Germans, and French. I traveled from Mozambique northward along the Indian Ocean shoreline to Tanzania, Kenya, and Somalia. Subject to the varied forces of their own histories, each was also unique in their modern incarnation. One of the few things they have always had in common is malaria, a mosquito-borne disease caused by a parasite which causes close to a million deaths every year, the majority of them in Africa. Another thing they share is a colonial heritage.

Mozambique is still struggling to emerge from a catastrophic civil war that began shortly after it won independence in the mid-seventies and lasted until 1992. Tanzania is still suffering from the effects of some of the socialist policies of its former President Julius Nyerere. Somalia remains at war with itself after more than twenty years of continuous bloodshed. And Kenya—my home for so many years—the longtime poster child for political stability in Africa, is an increasingly violent place that is heading toward an increasingly uncertain future. None are entirely free of the collective traumas of their colonial pasts, but most have already succumbed to the embrace of a powerful and wealthy newcomer from abroad—China.

Mosquito Coast is a visual notebook of all of this, and also a repository of memory.

I wanted to capture the last vestiges of the twentieth century in a unique part of Africa before they disappear forever. After a hundred years of being shaped violently by colonial powers, by Cold War politics, by proxy wars between East and West, a monster has emerged in the form of religious radicalism. There is no discernable end to this story yet. The jihadi fighters in Somalia and Kenya may overwrite the old histories with their actions, or they will eventually be seen off, as the European colonizers once were. In the meantime, I wanted to leave a record of a place still caught in time, a place which, like a love lost, remains very special to me.

GUILLAUME BONN

Near the beginning of *A Bend in the River,* V. S. Naipaul's magisterial novel about Africa, his narrator, Salim, a trader of Muslim Indian heritage, tries to explain his peculiar sense of identity:

> *Africa was my home, had been the home of my family for centuries. But we came from the east coast, and that made the difference. The coast was not truly African. It was an Arab-Indian-Persian-Portuguese place, and we who lived there were really people of the Indian Ocean. True Africa was at our back . . . we looked east to the lands with which we traded—Arabia, India, Persia. These were also the lands of our ancestors. But we could no longer say that we were Arabians or Indians or Persians; when we compared ourselves with these people, we felt like people of Africa.*[1]

Salim's Africa begins on the Horn where the Red Sea opens out to the Indian Ocean in front of the enclave of Djibouti, opposite Yemen. Heading southward, it takes in Somaliland, Somalia, and then Kenya and Tanzania with their offshore islands of Lamu and Zanzibar respectively, continuing all the way down to where Mozambique meets South Africa and is buttressed seaward by the great island of Madagascar. That is where Guillaume Bonn was born, as were his father and grandfather before him. Bonn's own heritage is colonial French, but his feelings of deep attachment to the same stretch of coast are uncannily similar to those of the fictional Salim.

In this book, Bonn has called that eastern African coast the "Mosquito Coast," because of the malarial curse shared by the four countries—Mozambique, Tanzania, Kenya, and Somalia—whose coastlines he has documented. The Arabs, history's great slavers, called it the "heathen coast." It could also be called the Swahili coast, for its polyglot lingua franca, or the monsoon coast, because it is along this coast that sailors of dhows originating out of Yemen, Oman, and from as far away as Persia and India, have sailed with the seasonal monsoon winds between Asia and Africa since time immemorial. Traditionally, the dhows carried cargoes of salt, livestock, pots, and tiles to Africa, and once there, loaded up cargoes of slaves, ivory, skins, shells, cloves, and mangrove timber. Over the centuries, little changed, except for some of the commodities traded. With the British ban on slavery in 1807 came six decades of gunboat diplomacy in the Indian Ocean as the Royal Navy sought to enforce the prohibition internationally; despite these efforts, Zanzibar remained East Africa's premier slaving port, into the eighteen-seventies.

With the so-called Scramble for Africa, from 1881 to 1914, involving the continent's wholesale colonization by a handful of European powers, East Africa's surviving tribal kingdoms and sultanates were conquered and colonized in a time span of little more than thirty years. Over the next half-century, through both world wars, most of Africa continued under colonial rule. Some of the colonies traded hands. German East Africa, comprising present-day Tanzania and Zanzibar, was transferred to British dominion after World War I, while Italy lost its colony of Italian Somaliland, also to the British, in World War II.

The nineteen-sixties brought independence and dramatic change to most of Africa. The first to become free on "the Coast" was Somalia, in 1960, uniting both former British and Italian colonies into one nation. Kenya's independence came in 1963, but only after the violent Mau-Mau rebellion, and the brutal counterinsurgency campaign the British waged to suppress it between 1952 and 1959. Tanzania and Zanzibar won their independence separately, in 1961 and 1963, and then joined to form a single nation in 1964. The longest-held of the European colonies, such as Mozambique, which had been governed by the Portuguese since 1505, were bitterly fought over, however, and were amongst the last to be freed. Despite more than a decade of armed revolt, Mozambique did not gain its independence until 1975, when a democratic revolution in Lisbon brought an end to Portugal's colonial empire.

For many of the new nations, independence brought dictatorship and bloody civil strife. Within two years of the Portuguese departure, Mozambique succumbed to a vicious civil war that dragged on until the early nineties, leaving the country ravaged and a million of its people dead. In independent Tanzania, a two-decade-long effort to "build socialism" was largely mayhem-free but ushered in a period of prolonged political and economic stagnation. Zanzibar had a brief but bloody Marxist secessionist rebellion. Following its Mau-Mau upheaval, Kenya became a relatively stable nation, although one characterized by exceedingly corrupt rule at the hands of a succession of elected kleptocrats. In the seventies, Somalia waged a vicious territorial war with Ethiopia in the

Ogaden Desert and found itself fought over as a regional proxy by both the United States and the Soviet Union, trading loyalties with both. With the fall of its longtime dictator Mohamed Siad Barre in 1991, Somalia succumbed to vicious inter-clan warfare and warlordism, famine, a disastrous intervention by U.S. military forces, and its disintegration into anarchy as the modern world's ultimate failed state.

Guillaume Bonn was raised in this newly independent African firmament. Born in Antananarivo, Madagascar, in 1970, he spent his early childhood there and in the nearby Comoros Islands—a French possession just then gaining partial independence, but with coups and revolts yet to come. That was followed by several years in former French Somaliland, by then called French Territory of Afars and the Issas, which gained independence in 1977 while he lived there and then became known as Djibouti. Bonn was fifteen when his family moved to Kenya. They stayed for seven years. He felt at home there, and although his parents eventually moved on, Bonn has remained attached to Kenya, and to Africa, ever since. Africa is where he finds his inspiration, and where he continues to live most of the time.

For Bonn, some of these countries evoke a bittersweet nostalgia for past times. His feelings for Somalia are different. Bonn once told me about a 1988 holiday with his father to Mogadishu, where the Bonns had family friends. It was a peaceful country then, and he loved it, recalling most of all its blinding sunlight and the iridescent blue of its sea. The next time he visited, in 1991, the peace had been broken. Siad Barre had just fallen from power, and all the foreign expats had fled Mogadishu. Bonn saw his first dead person lying in the street. Two years later, in Bonn's first assignment as a photojournalist, he returned to Mogadishu to cover the ill-fated U.S. intervention called "Operation Restore Hope." To report on the crisis, he joined up with his best friend, a young American journalist named Dan Eldon. On July 12, 1993, a few weeks after Bonn left Mogadishu, Eldon was beaten and stabbed to death, along with two colleagues, by an angry mob. Bonn did not return to Somali for many years afterward.

In one of the most iconic pictures in this book, a group of idle men stand or sit amongst a few fishing boats beached amidst the ruins of stone buildings in Mogadishu's ancient seafront district known as Hamerwene.

Some are looking silently out to sea, while others appear to be talking amongst themselves. All of them seem to be waiting for something, but they do not resemble Englishmen, anxiously waiting for a bus to come. These men are not in a hurry.

All along the Mosquito Coast, Africans subsist timelessly in a kind of existential limbo, eking out their lives amidst the wreckage of lost civilizations. In many places, nothing has yet come along to replace them. In Beira, we see abandoned nightclubs, golf clubs, and hotels, proof that there was a time before, in which other, more prosperous people once lived there—people who had time for things like recreation. In the blackened cavity of a long-since abandoned Olympic-sized swimming pool, a woman squats at the water's edge, washing clothes. The one-time luxury hotel behind her is now a squalid tenement for poor people like herself. In Mogadishu, on her way from one place to another, a Somali woman in a red robe and matching turban takes a shortcut through the archway of the bombed-out husk of the old Italian cathedral. In Tanga, a librarian sits at a desk that is overlooked by a bronze bust of the late British King George VI, still there after all these years.

Like an archaeologist, Bonn's urge is to seek out and preserve whatever amounts to a legacy of the past in East Africa. The difference is that he takes pictures, and what vestigial presence there is, the past in East Africa is recent. Colonial Africa came and went in a lifetime, and its remains are tumbledown train stations, soldiers' barracks, and churches, but also cinemas, bars, and yacht harbors, made not out of gracious stone, but limewashed concrete.

Occasionally, we see glimpses of a new Africa. It is mostly Chinese-built, quickly erected and overwhelming in scale, seemingly on the verge of sweeping the old life away—just as it has in China. Around the Tanzanian capital of Dar es Salaam, new generic office towers and recently constructed apartment blocks have arisen above the older, smaller city. The vacant lots around them are rendered meaningless in the newly changed landscape; neither farmer's field nor building plot, they have become dead zones and, as such, are heaped with garbage. Such images are a reminder of the unevenness of life in Africa, and of how the price being paid for a notional modernity is the displacement of people and the eradication of the original environment.

In many of Bonn's images there is an air of bittersweet lamentation, but also, here and there, restorative glimpses of life going on. African families delightedly swim at a Maputo Beach, where there is still sun and sea and sand. Elsewhere, a colorful café fashioned out of an old movie theater caters to new guests. A smiling man collects seaweed on a beach.

Just as the epic Scramble for Africa took place over a mere three decades, the independence era lasted a mere fifteen years. Prolonged warfare has irrevocably altered countries like Somalia and Mozambique, while "peaceful" nations like Kenya and Tanzania have seen their wilderness areas and traditional rural ways of life devastated by rapid population growth and the birth of urban slums. In the past decade and a half, China's arrival in Africa has brought a boom in new development, including roadwork, railways, ports, dams, pipelines, industrial plants, and massive residential construction projects. In exchange, the Chinese have acquired mines and oil fields and forests and huge swathes of land for agribusiness. With this activity has come new wealth, but also widespread social and environmental disruption. Great new Chinese seaport construction projects are already underway on Kenya's coast at Lamu and Mombasa, at Bagamoyo in Tanzania, and at Pemba in Mozambique. It is all happening very fast, and it seems likely that within another fifteen years, much of Africa's Mosquito Coast will be unrecognizable.

A couple of years ago, I spent some time with Bonn in Kenya, and together we journeyed into the bush, to the far north of the country near the Ethiopian and Somali borders, and also to the south, close to the border with Tanzania. On the coast, things were tense: Somali gunmen had been raiding, kidnapping, and also murdering people. In Nairobi, traffic was snarled as Chinese construction firms built a new highway network, complete with bridges and flyovers to speed traffic across the city. As the modest colonial grid of roads was chewed up to make way for more lanes, the century-old jacaranda and thika trees that had once shaded them were being chopped down. We stayed in an outlying neighborhood of comfortable villas with large gardens which, just a few years before, had been surrounded by open bush. Now the city had mostly surrounded it. Even so, the local news was all about a wild lion on the prowl in the area. Armed guards stood at barricades here and there, and they confirmed the stories.

The news of the lion delighted Bonn, as it did me, momentarily quashing the feeling that Kenya, and the rest of Africa, was irretrievably doomed to succumb to the enervatingly generic suburbanization that has transformed so much of the world over the last half century. In spite of everything, the presence of the lion seemed to say that Africa was still Africa. But for how much longer? It is a question which, although unasked, runs throughout this book and is present in all of Bonn's work.

It has been his destiny to document the demise of the old ways and the natural environment of the continent that gave him birth. But the human upheaval he spends his life witnessing and recording is also his own. However much Bonn loves Africa, he is becoming inexorably displaced from it. The proof of life that was left behind by his forebears, and others like them, is vanishing quickly.

In *A Bend in the River,* Salim recalls a stockade on the beach of his East African hometown:

> *The walls were of brick. It was a ruin when I was a boy, and in tropical Africa, land of impermanent building, it was like a rare piece of history. It was in this stockade that the slaves were kept after they had been marched down from the interior in the caravans; there they waited for the dhows to take them across the sea. But if you didn't know, then the place was nothing, just four crumbling walls in a picture-postcard setting of beach and coconut trees.*[2]

There is an image in Guillaume Bonn's book which seems intimately related to Salim's observation. It shows three men playing with lifebuoys in pools of water in the rocky shoals of a coastline that had once been a major slave port. Except for Bonn's assertion, there is no stockade, nothing visible at all to tell of the terrible history that took place there, over many centuries, not so long ago.

Notes
1 V. S. Naipaul, *A Bend in the River* (London, 2011), p. 12.
2 Ibid., pp. 13–14.

MOZAMBIQUE

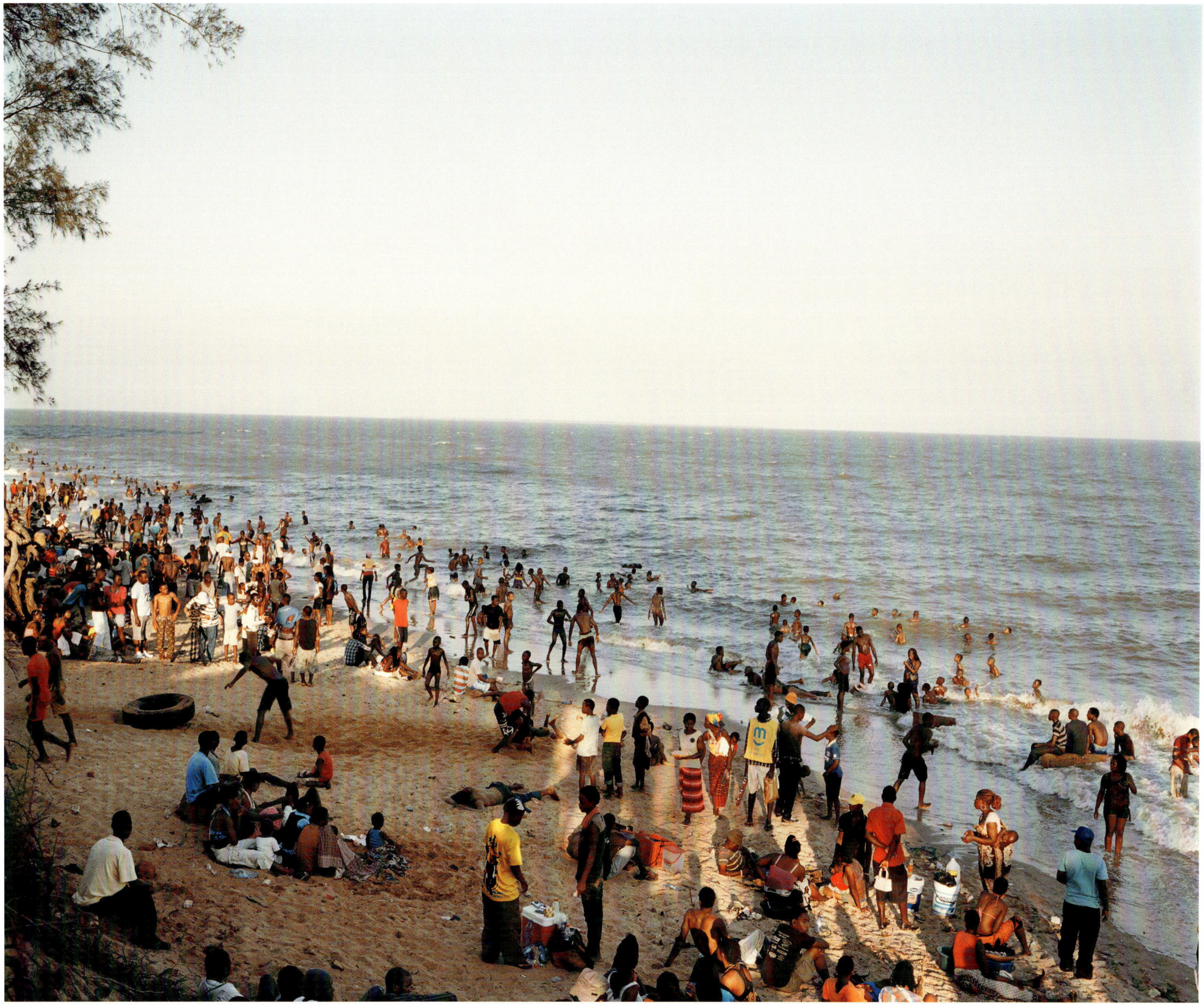

Public beach, Maputo, 2011

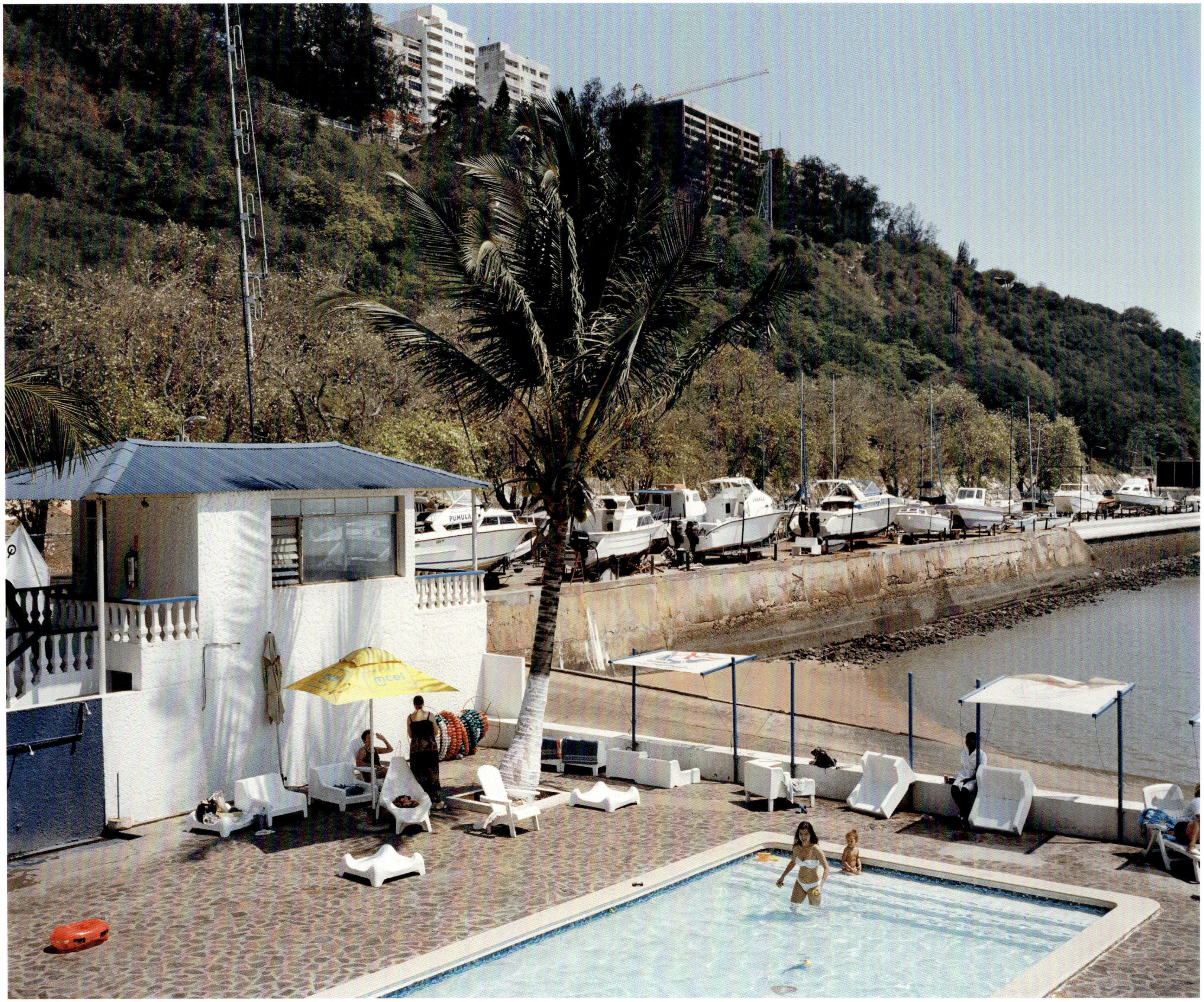

Clube Naval, Maputo, 2011

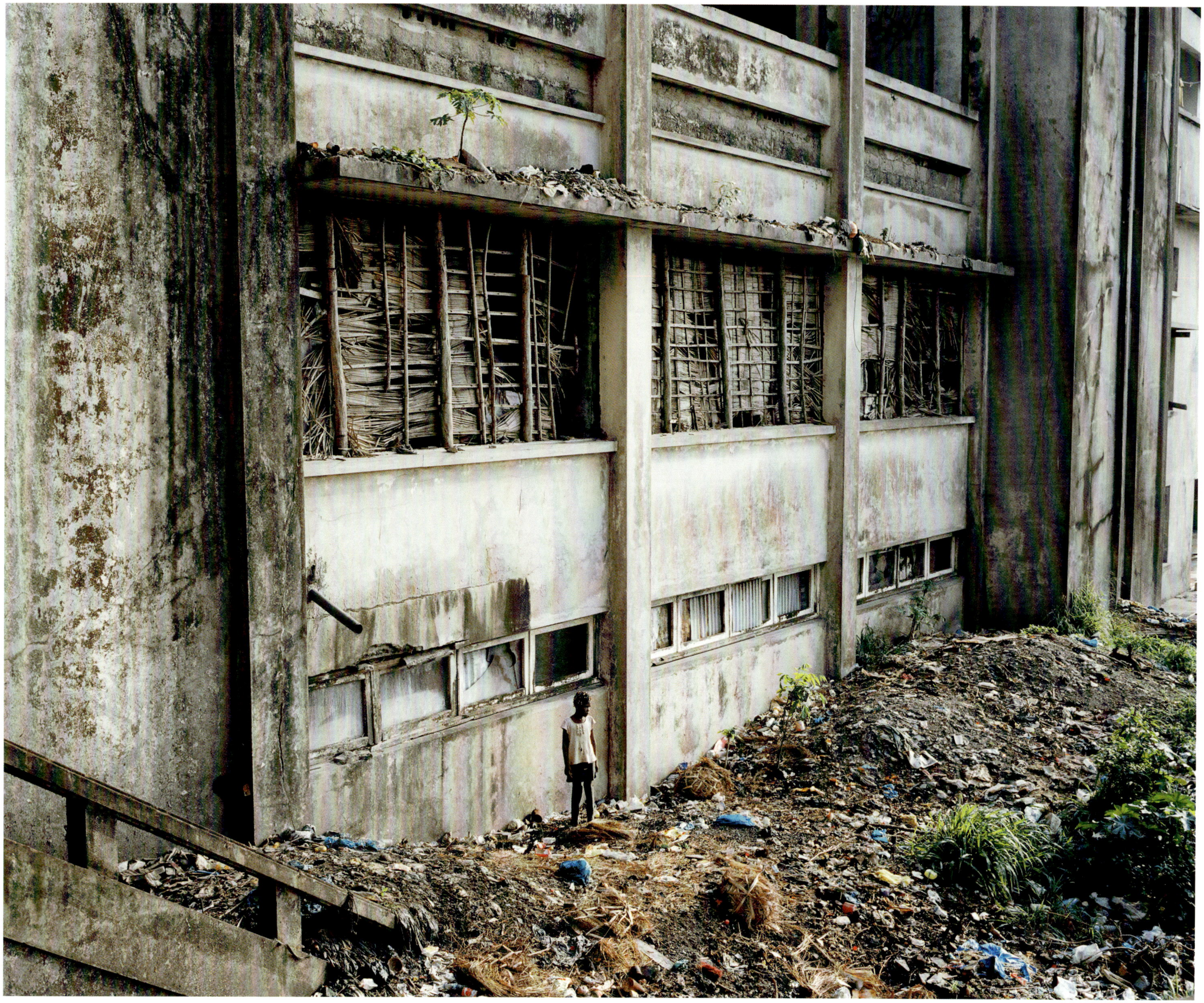

Apartment building, Mateus Sansão Muthemba Avenue, Beira, 2012

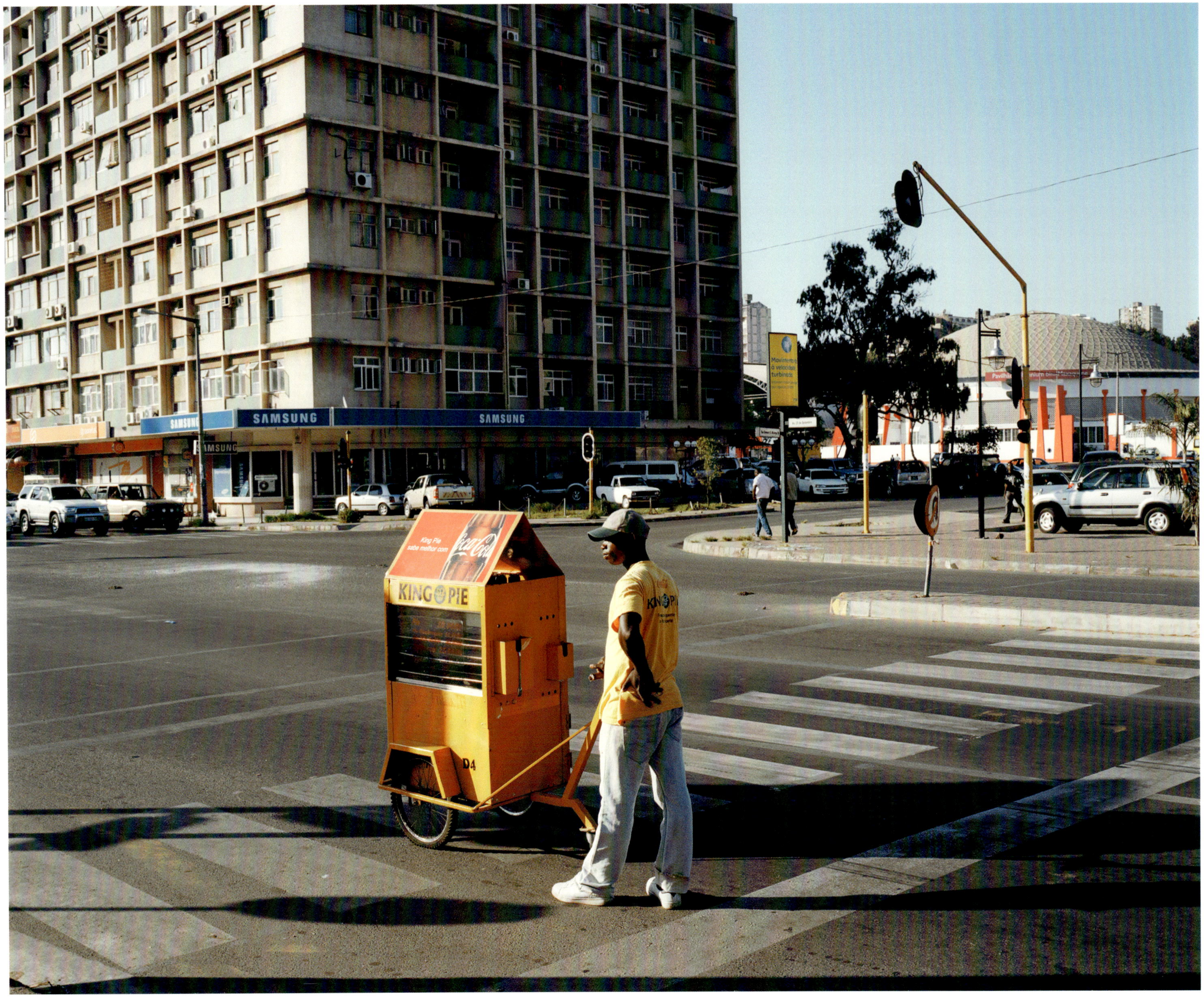

Ambulant food vendor, Maputo, 2011

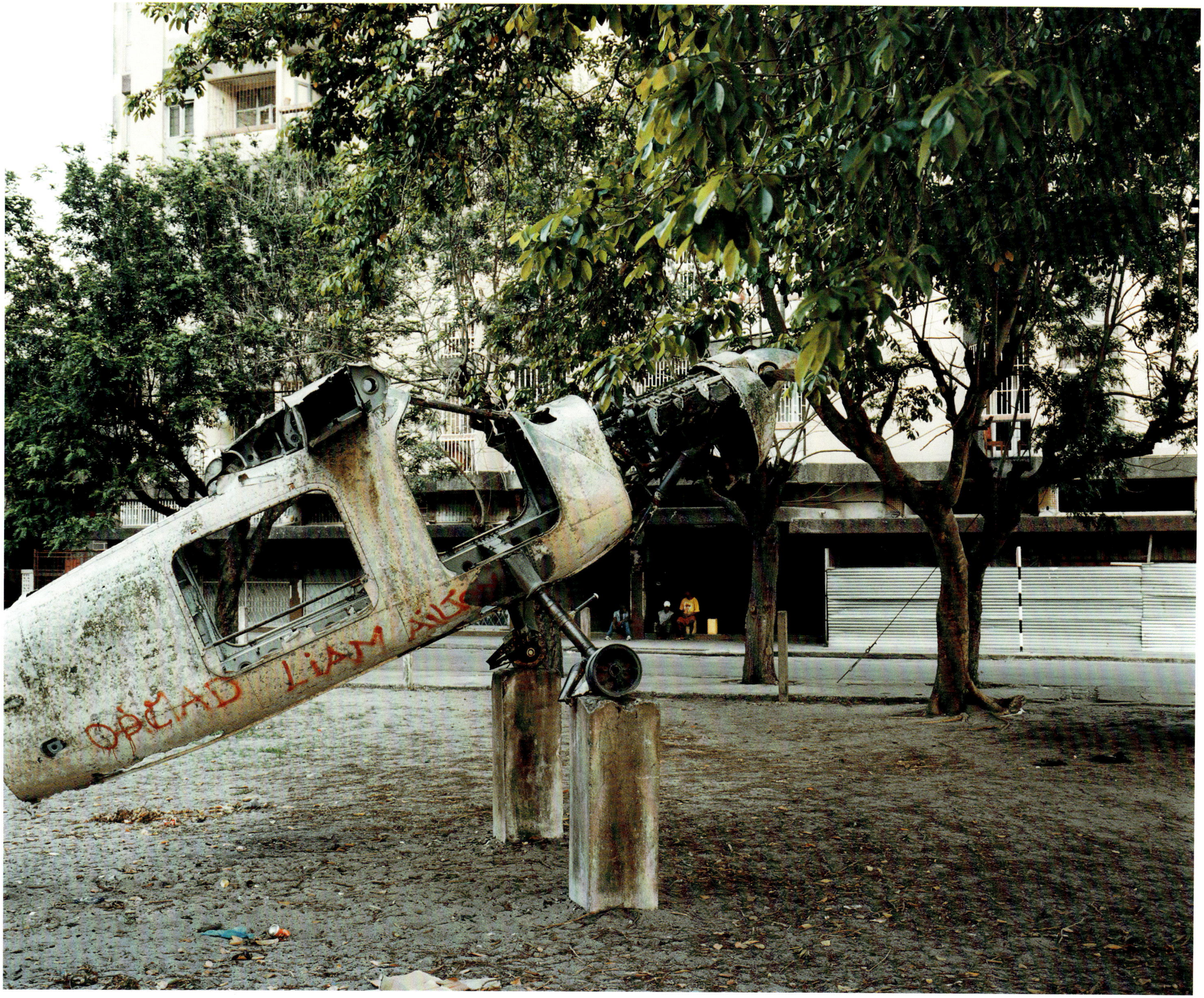

War relic turned sculpture, Beira, 2012

I knew the Grande Hotel from pictures, and I always knew that one day I would see it for real. During the nineteen-fifties and sixties, before Mozambique won its independence, Beira was a playground for rich white Rhodesians and South Africans; now it feels like a city frozen in time, forgotten by the rest of the world. I drove around, looking for the hotel, and then suddenly there it was. When it first opened its doors in the fifties, the Grande Hotel was billed as the "Pride of Africa," the largest and most modern hotel on the continent, an architectural triumph, a monument to parquet, marble, and glass with sweeping views of the Indian Ocean. Yet within a decade it had shut its doors, unable to turn a profit. In the late seventies, civil war broke out in Mozambique and the hotel became a refugee camp. When the war ended, many people simply stayed on. It is now home to some 3,500 squatters. The Grande Hotel stands as a reminder of an age of insouciance that is gone forever. Mozambique has emerged from civil war as one of the world's fastest growing economies, with investment in oil, gas, coal, and titanium. But its infrastructure is abysmal, and more than half of the population still scrapes by on less than one dollar a day.

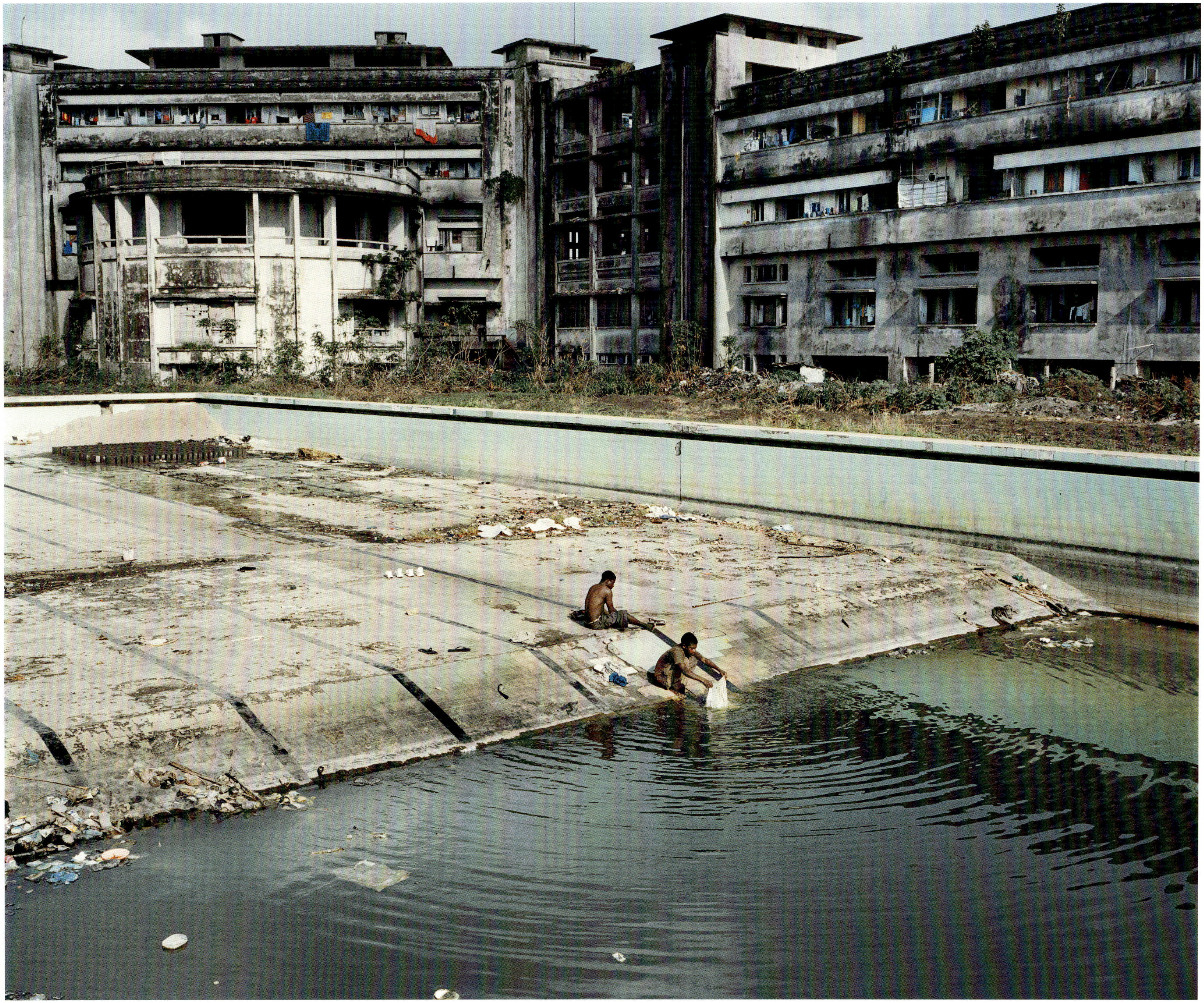

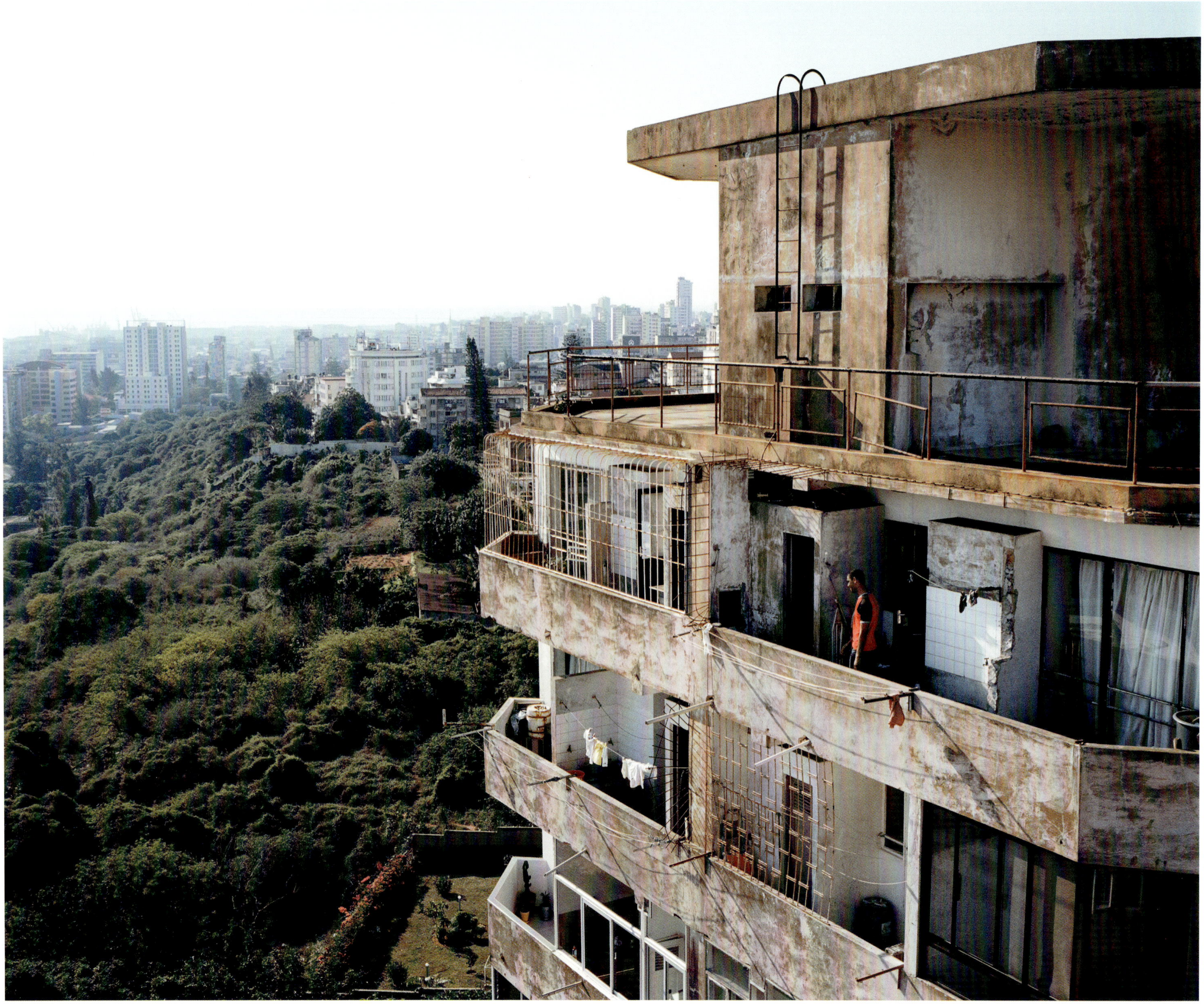

Apartment building near Almeida Ribeiro Avenue, Maputo, 2011

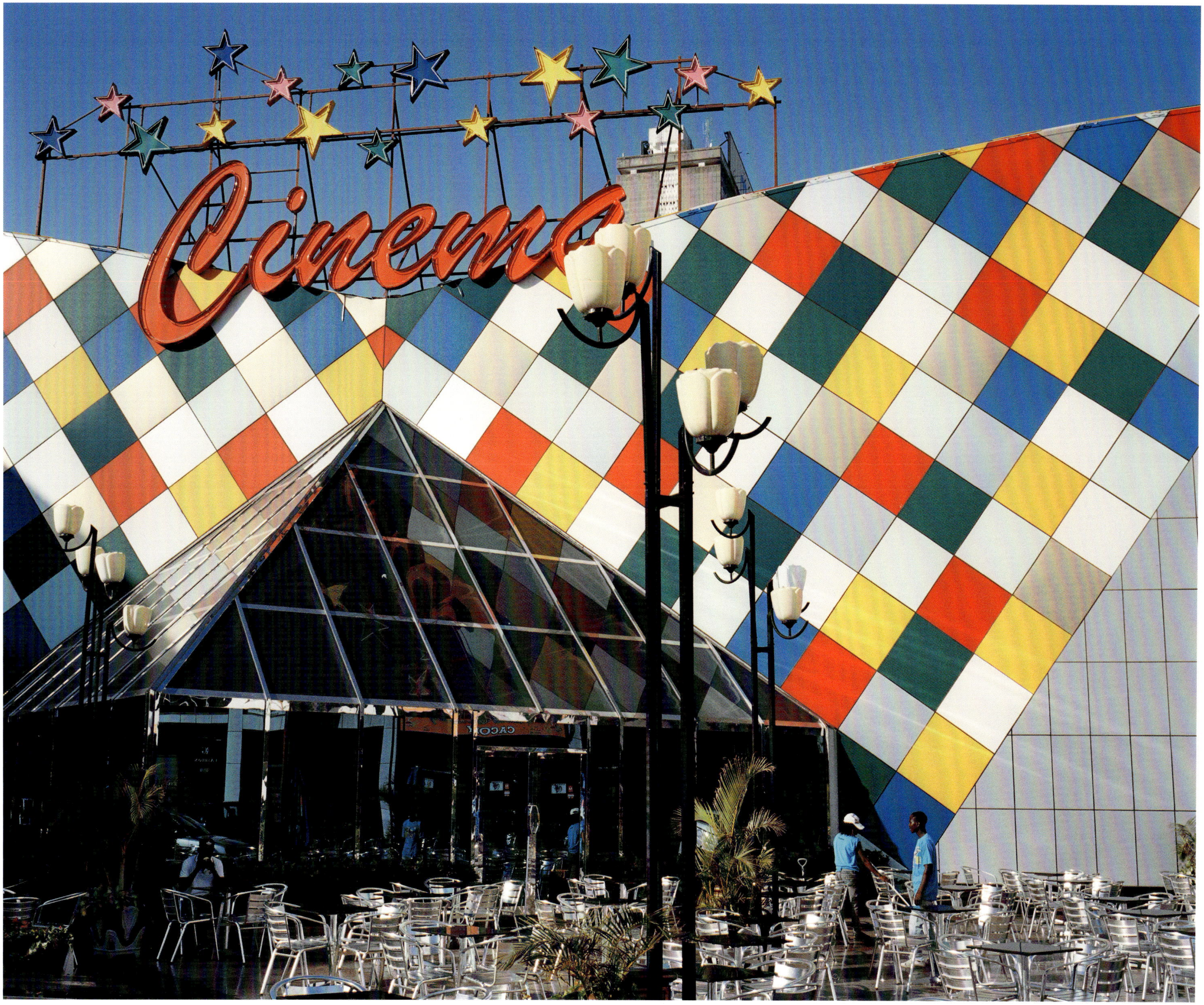

Shopping mall, Maputo, 2012

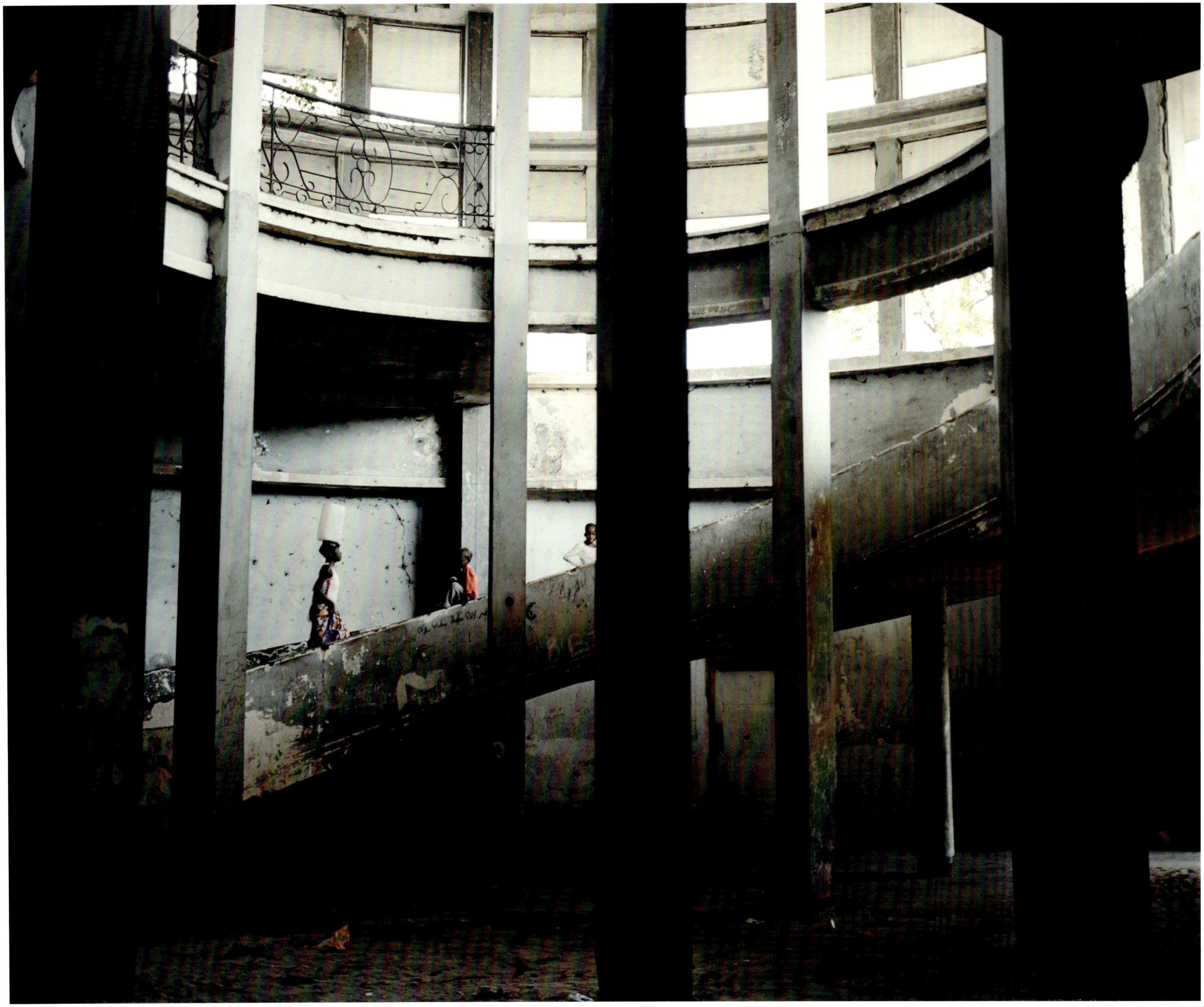

Once the lobby of the Grande Hotel, Beira, 2012

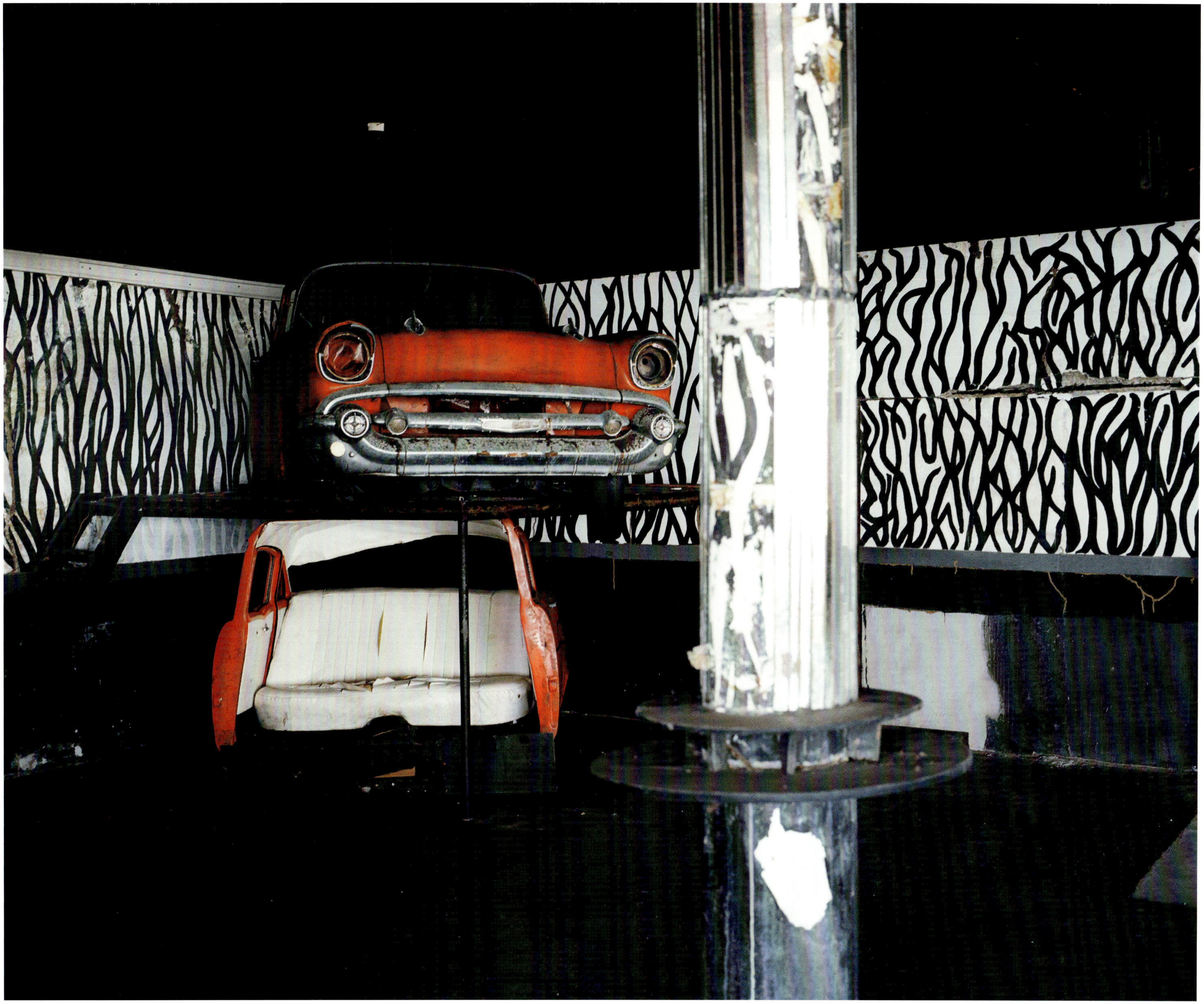

Abandoned nightclub, Beira, 2012

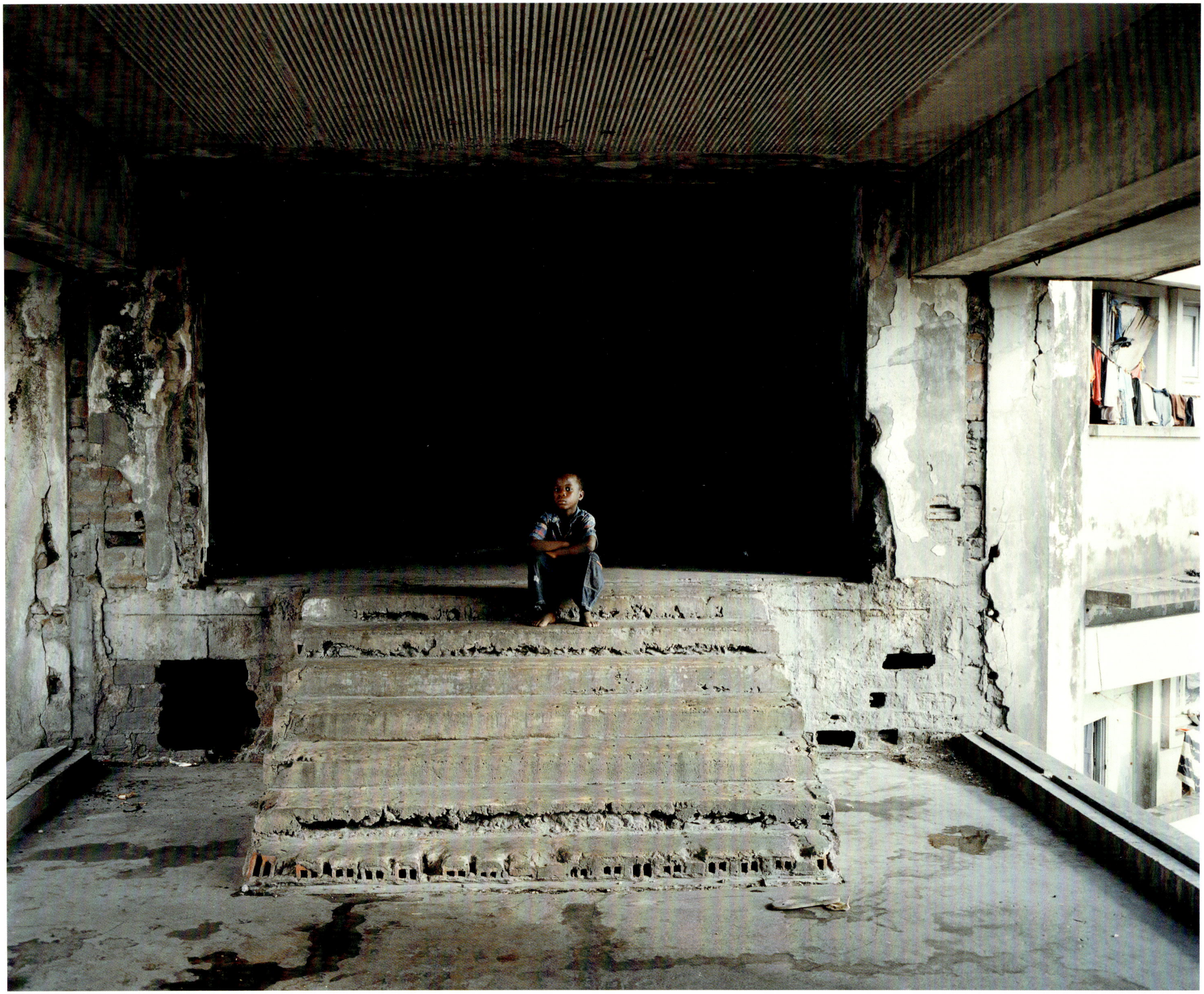

Apartment building, Beira, 2012

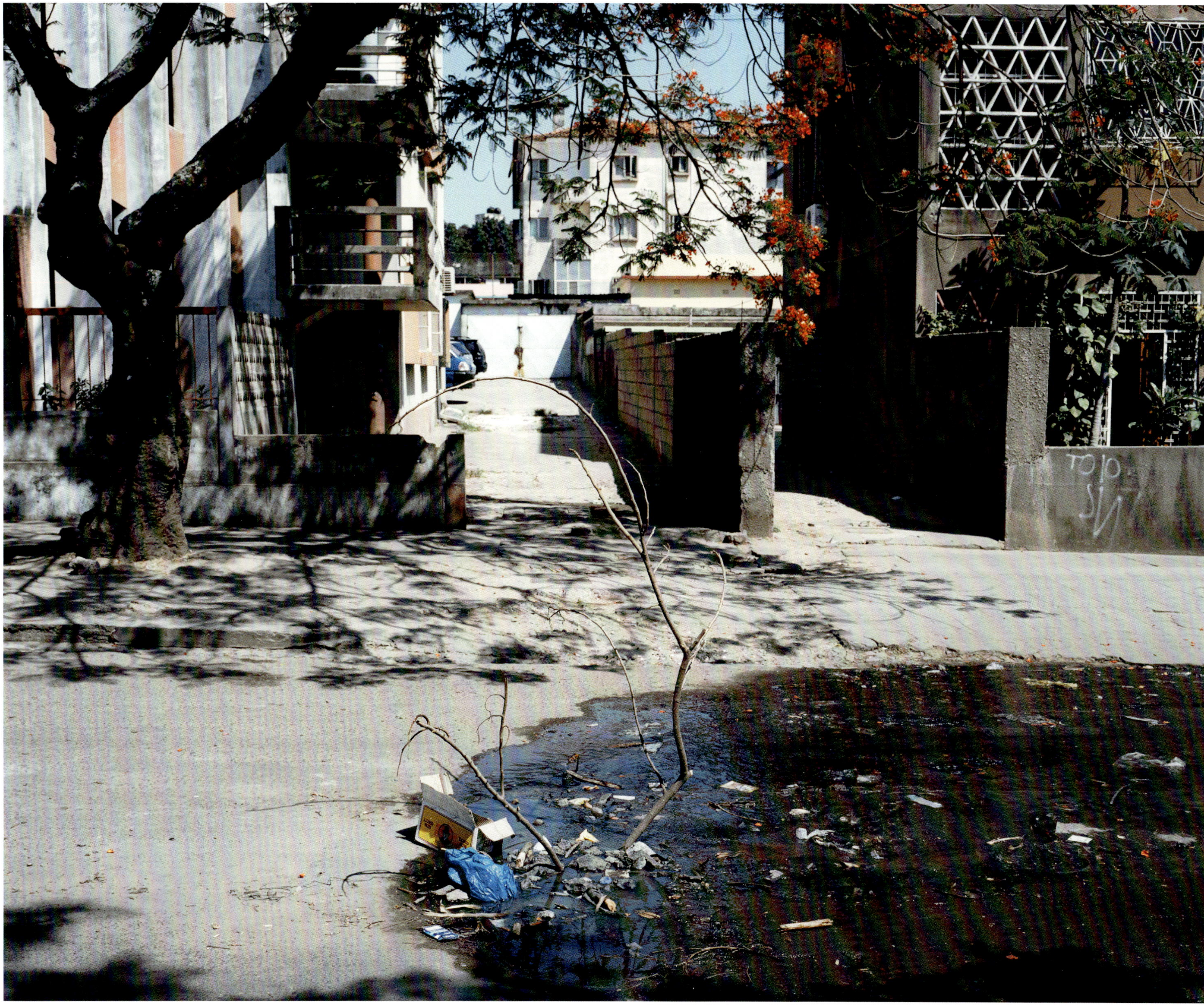

Tree branch turned into a street sign indicating a deep water hole, Maputo, 2011

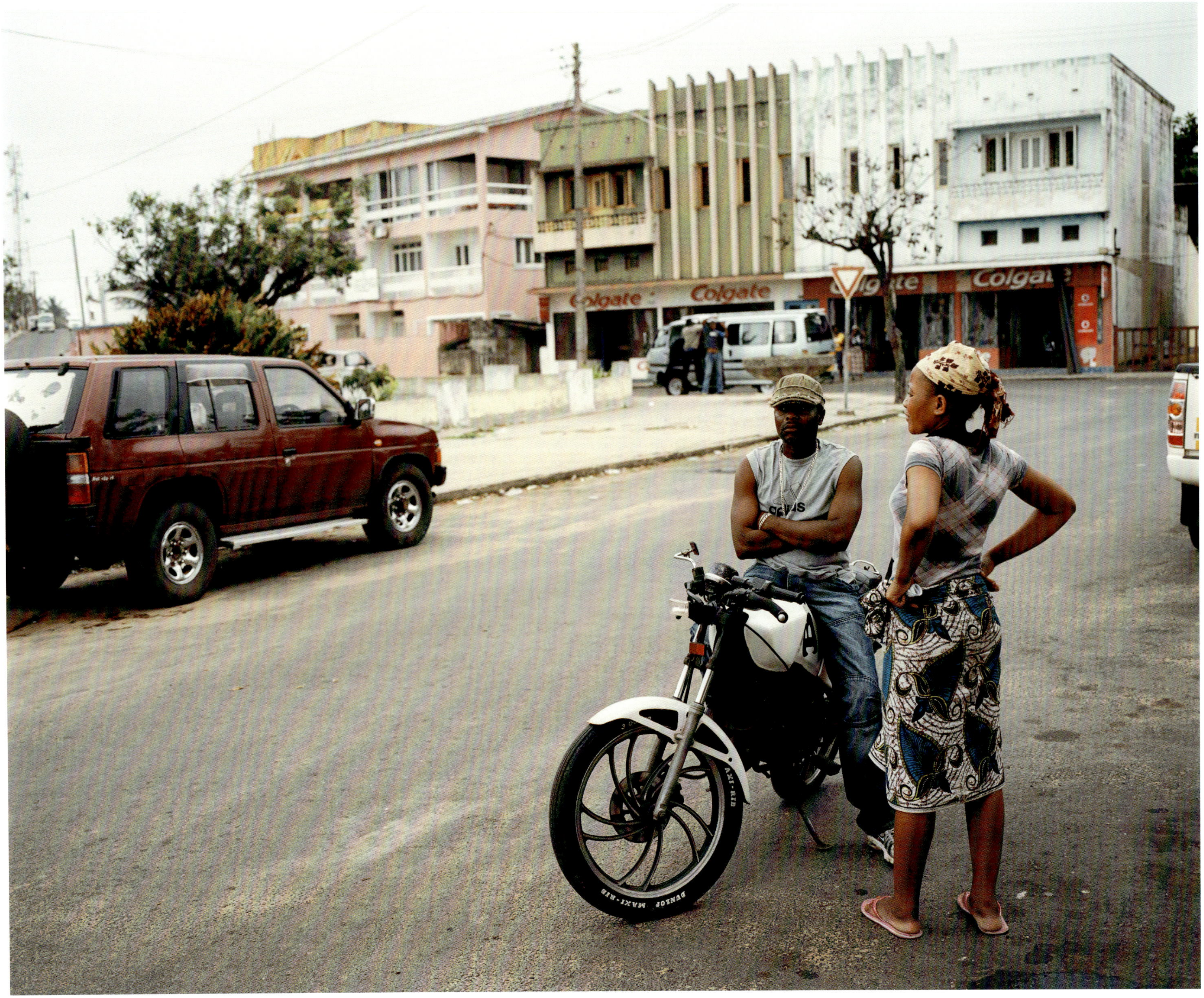

Near Moamed Sékou Touré Street, Inhambane, 2012

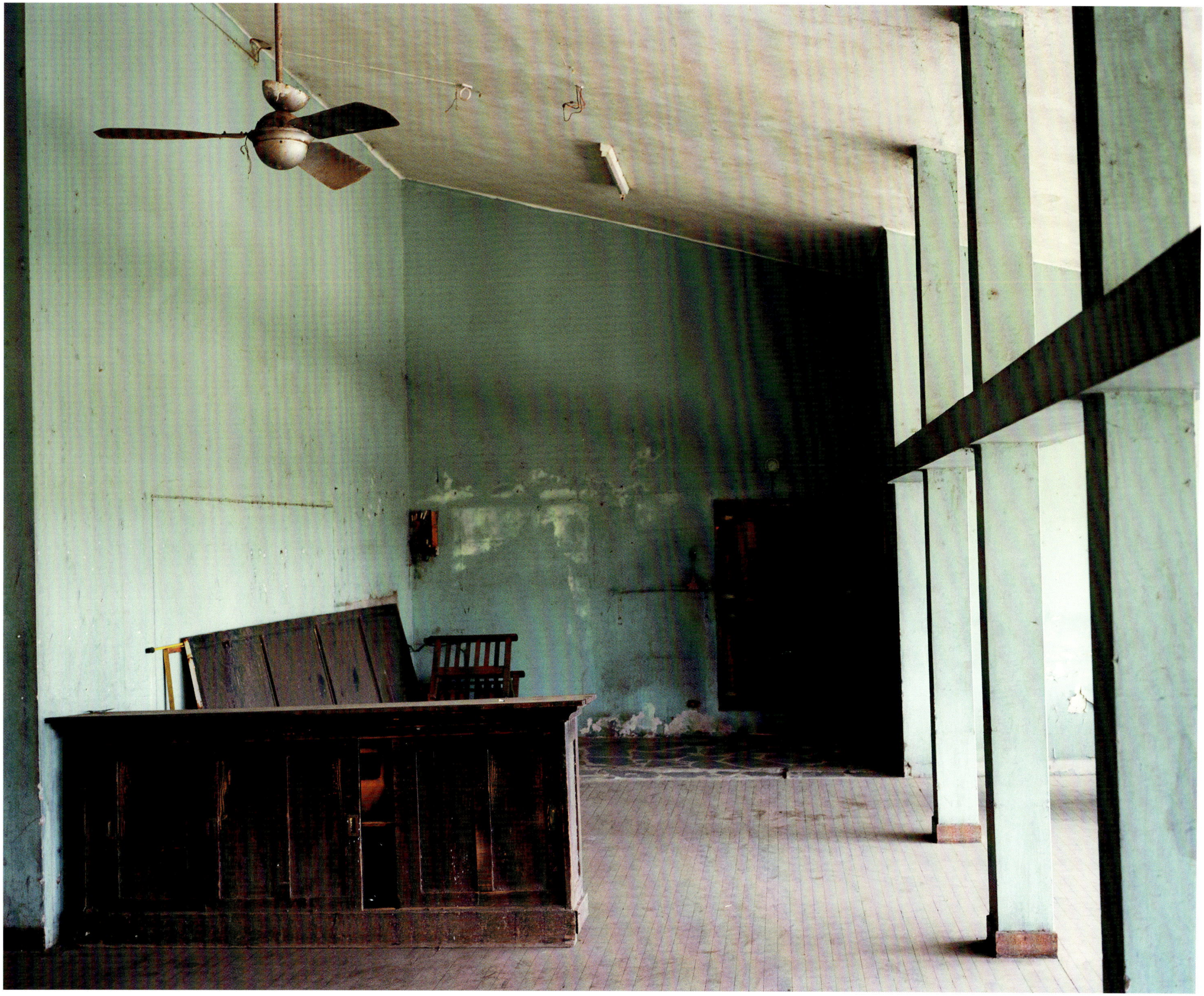

The old colonial golf club, Maputo, 2011

Restaurante Clube Nautico, Beira, 2012

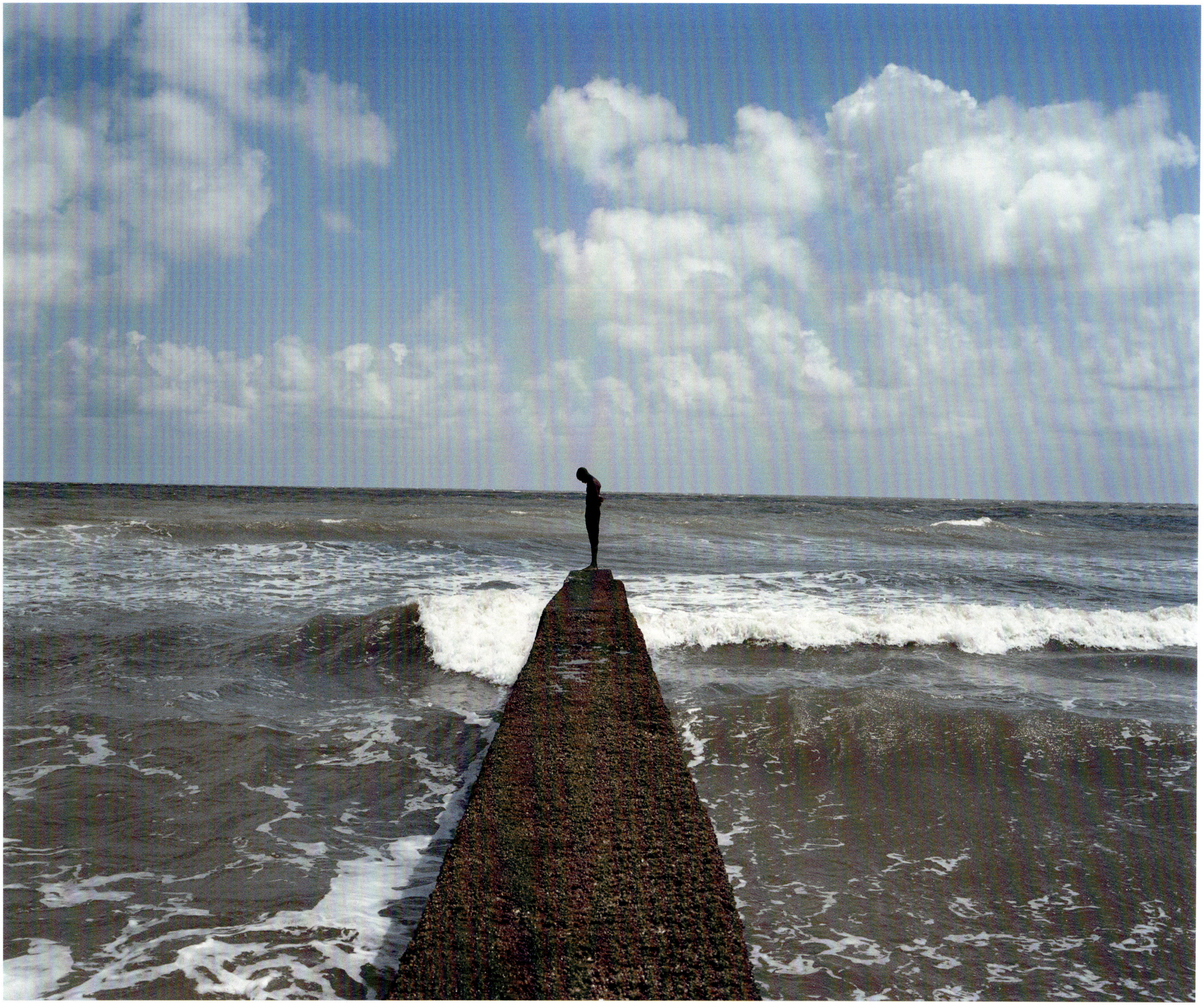

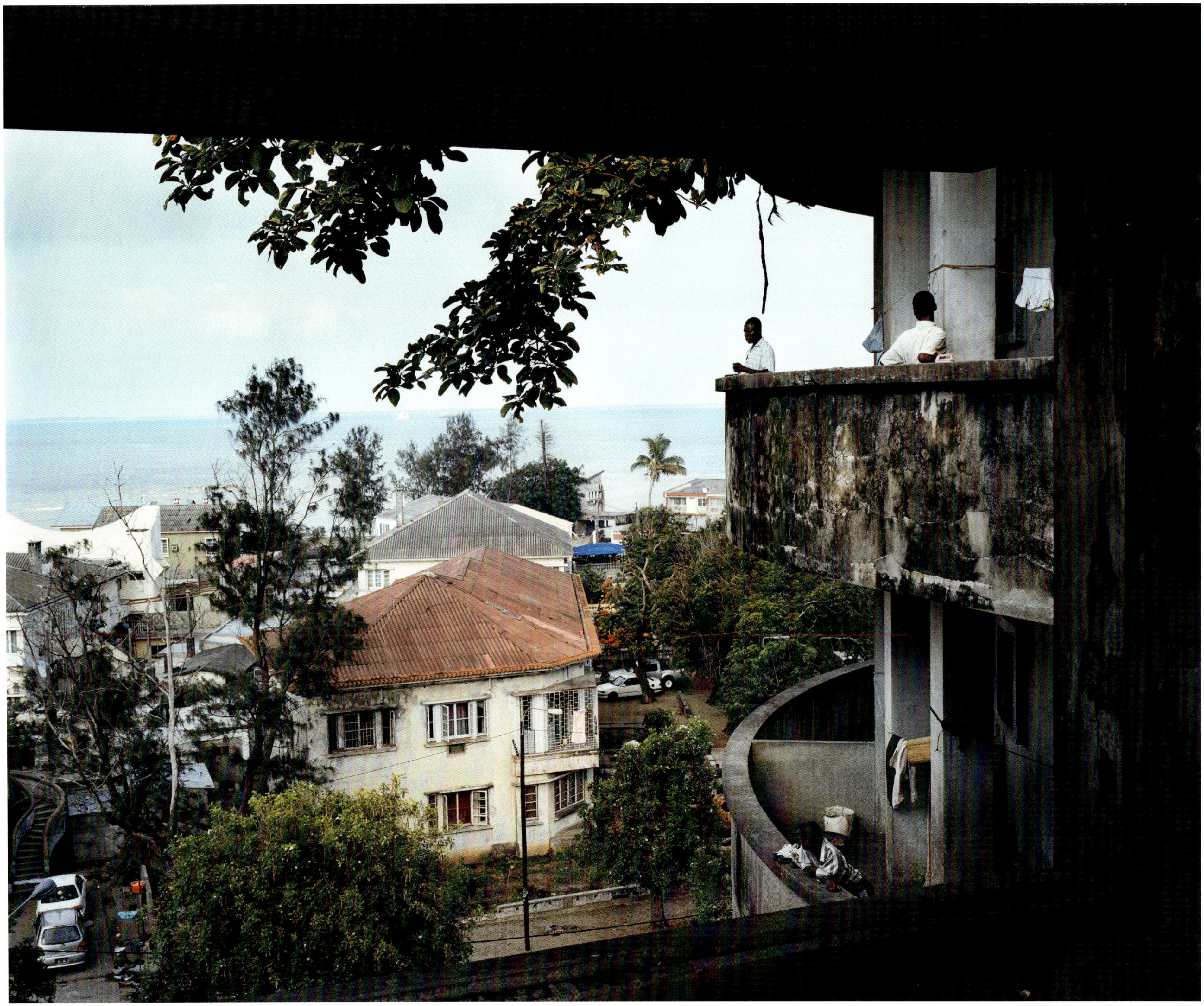

Apartment building now occupied by squatters, Beira, 2012

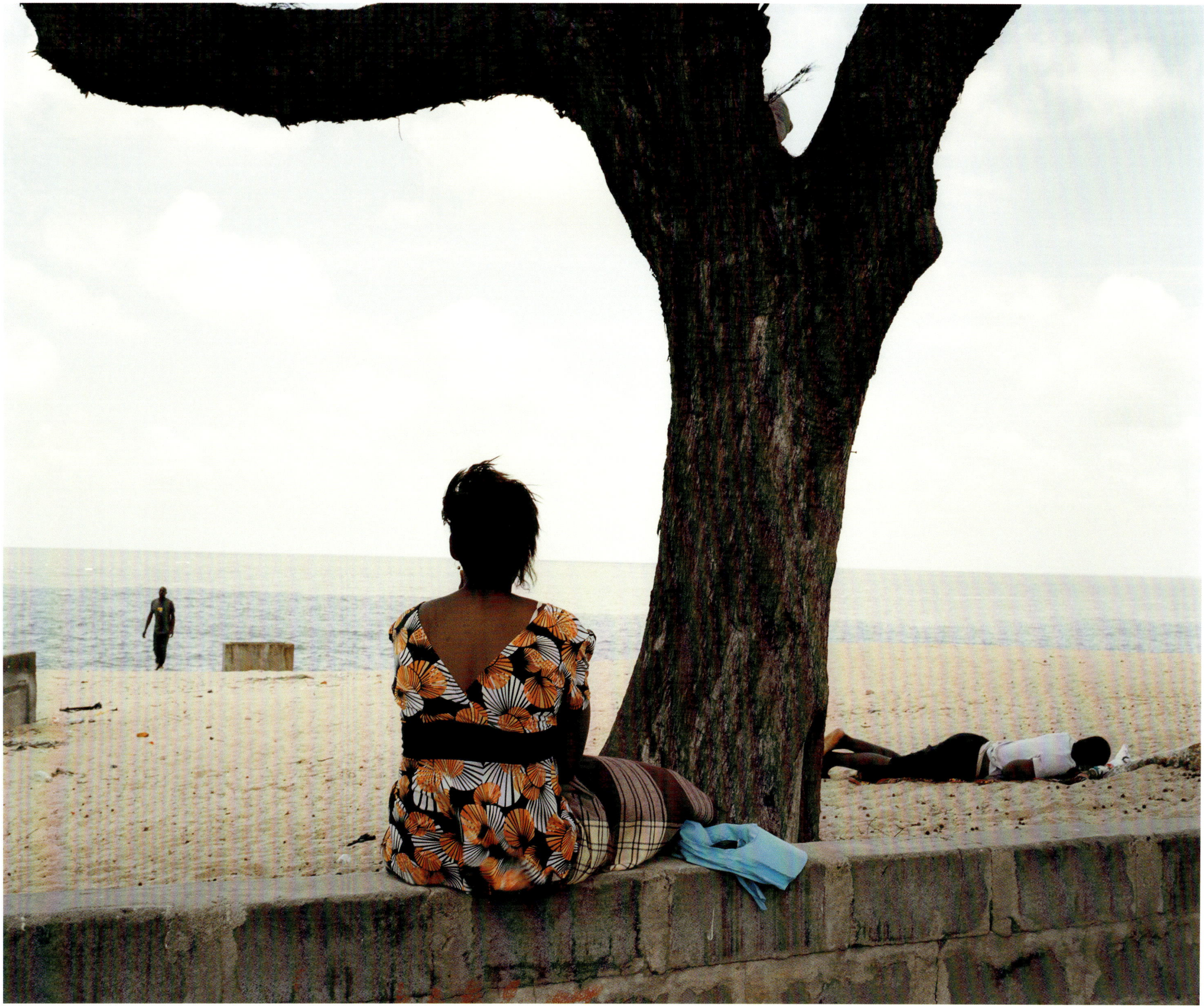

Avenidas das FPLM, Beira, 2012

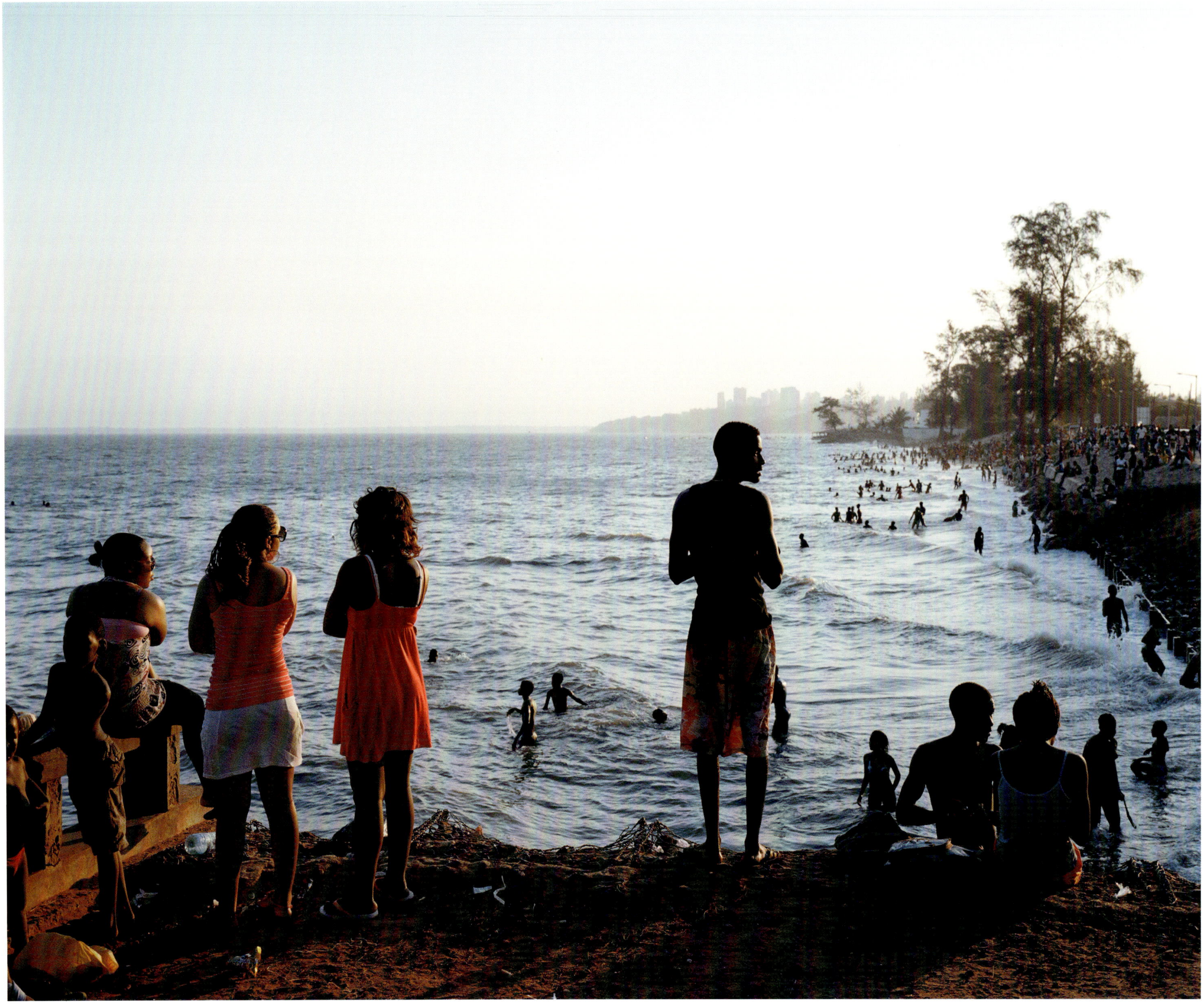

Public beach, Maputo, 2011

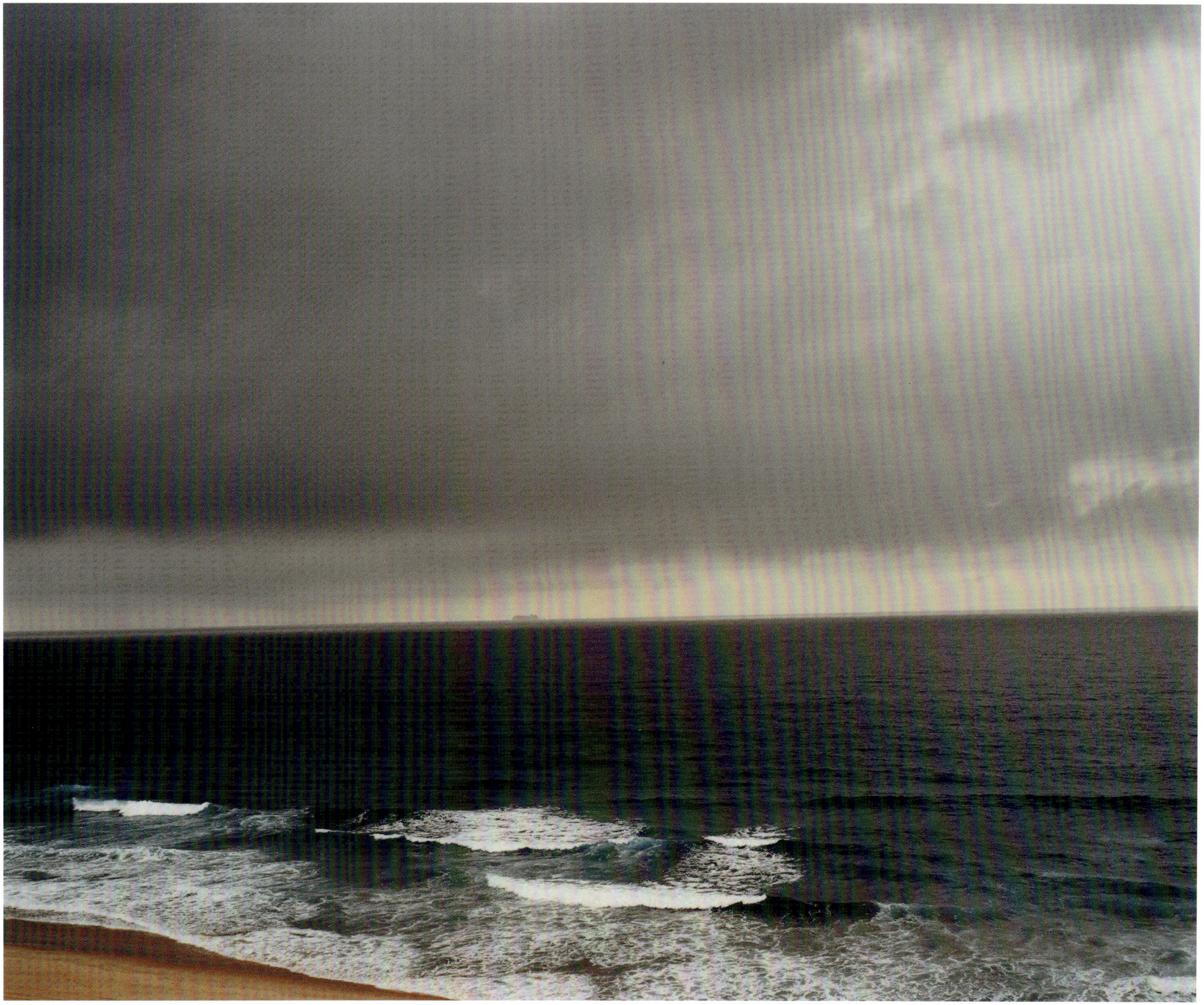

Guinjata Bay, 2012

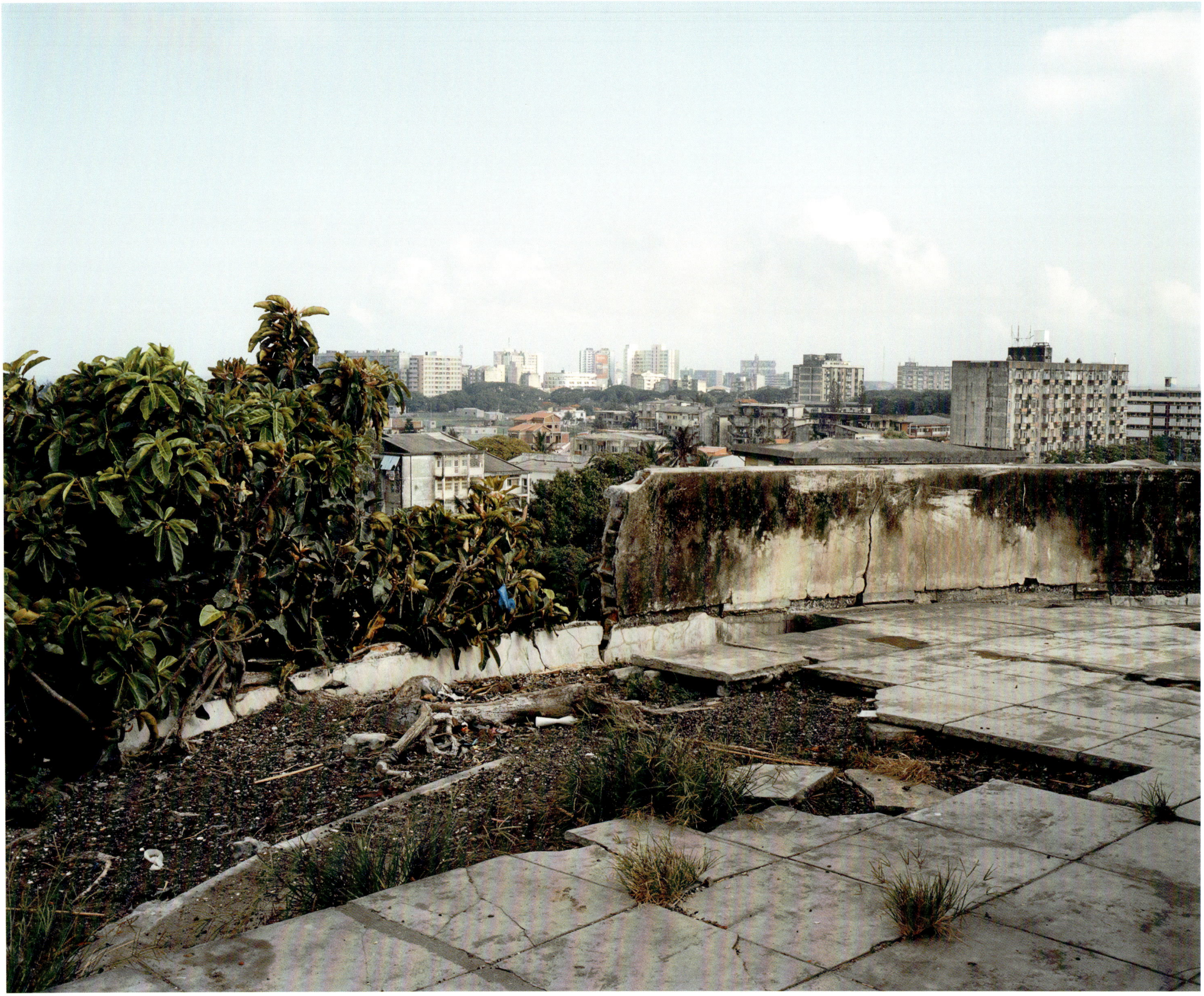

View of downtown Beira, 2012

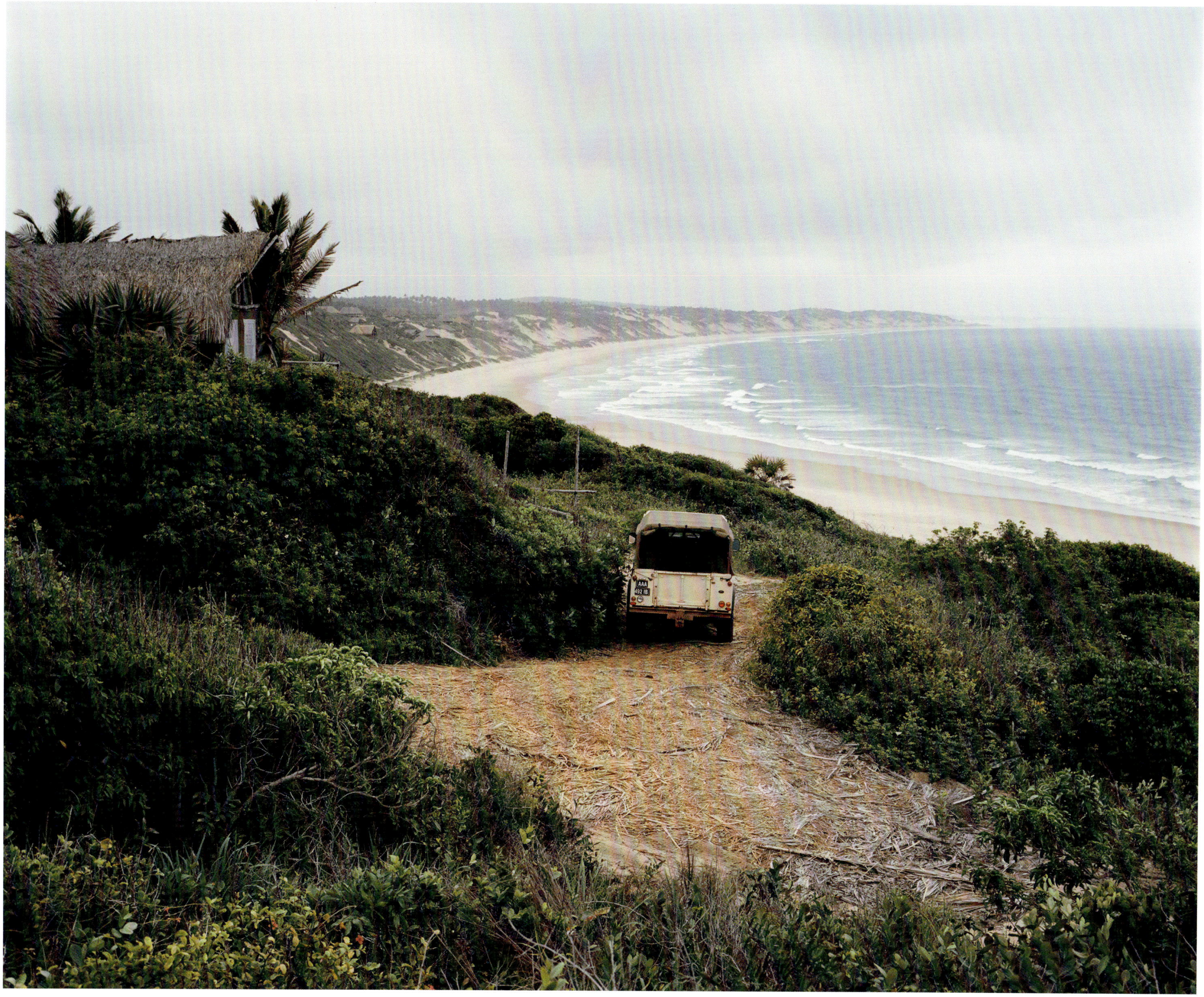

Guinjata Bay, 2012

TANZANIA

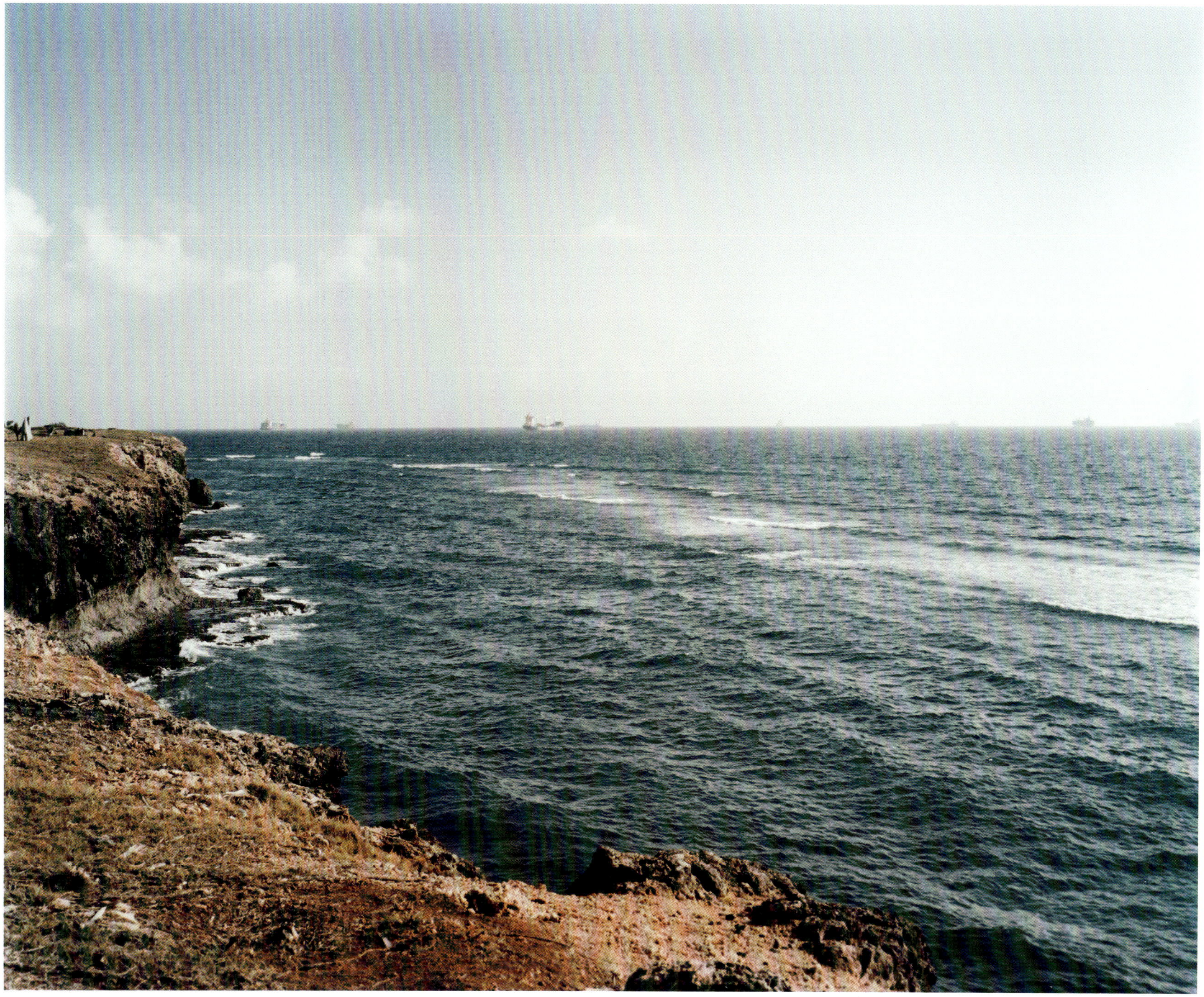

Merchant ships waiting to enter the port of Dar es Salaam, 2011

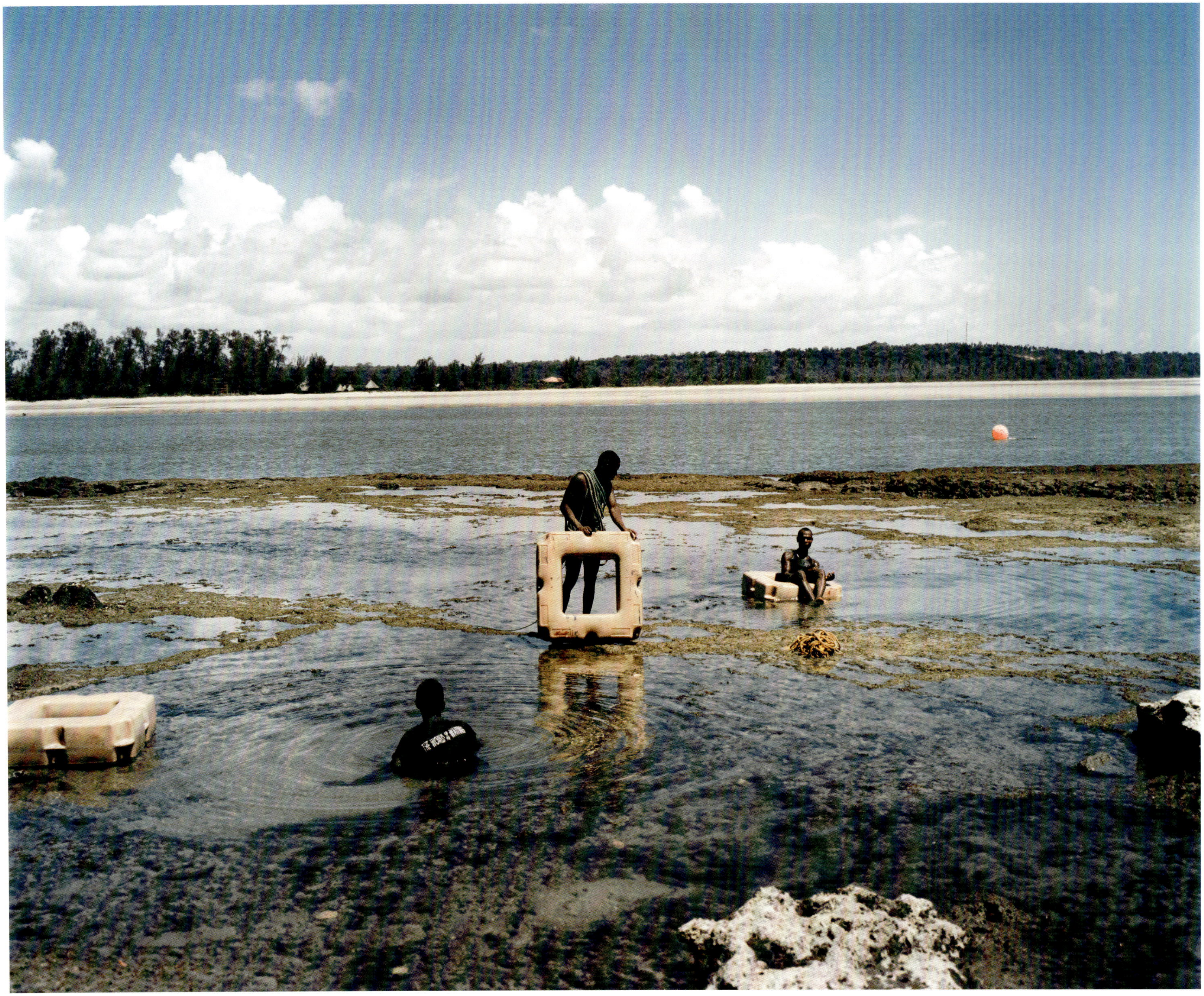

Where the Pangani River meets the Indian Ocean, an area that was once an important center of the slave trade, 2011

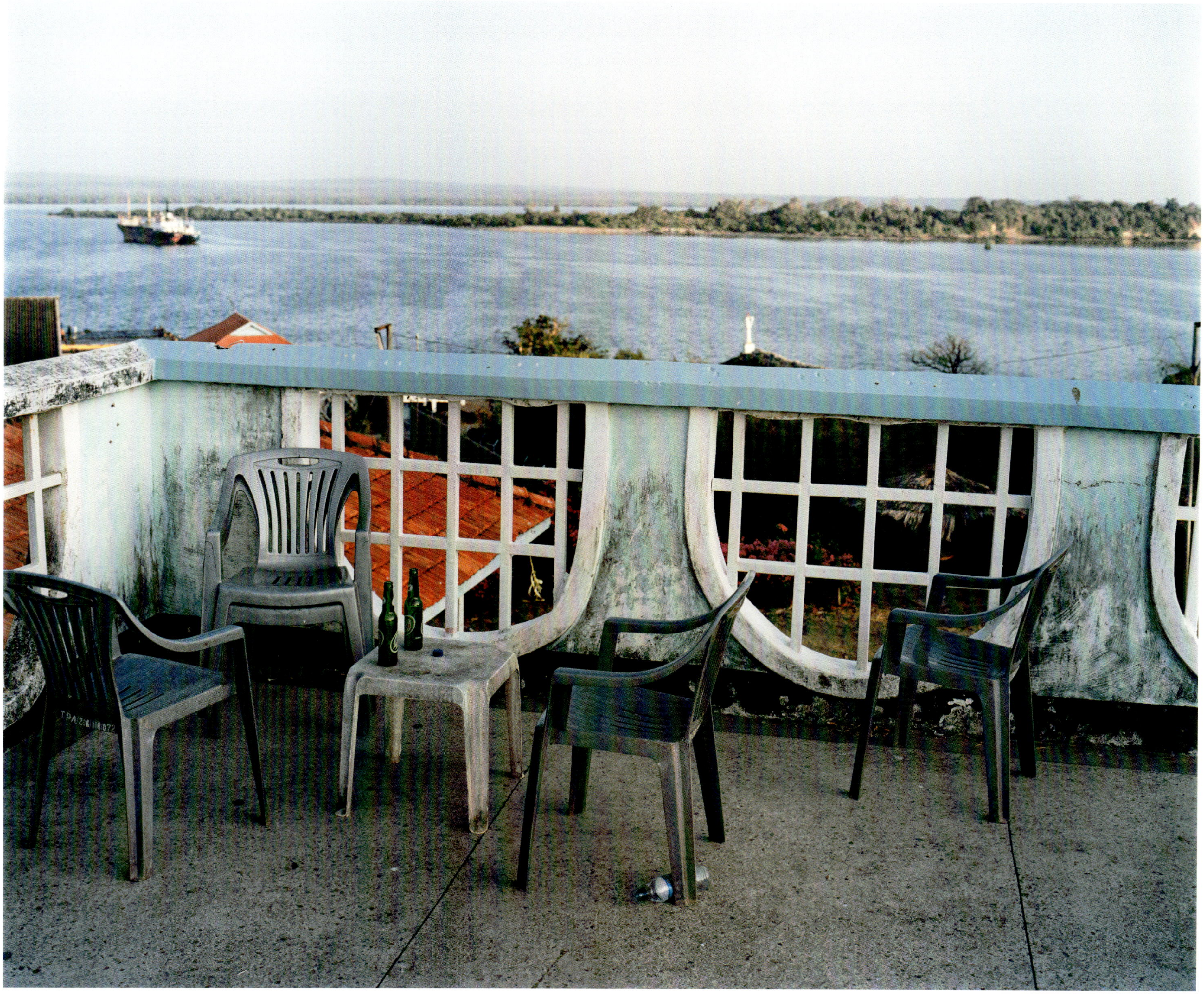

Tanga's harbor, 2011

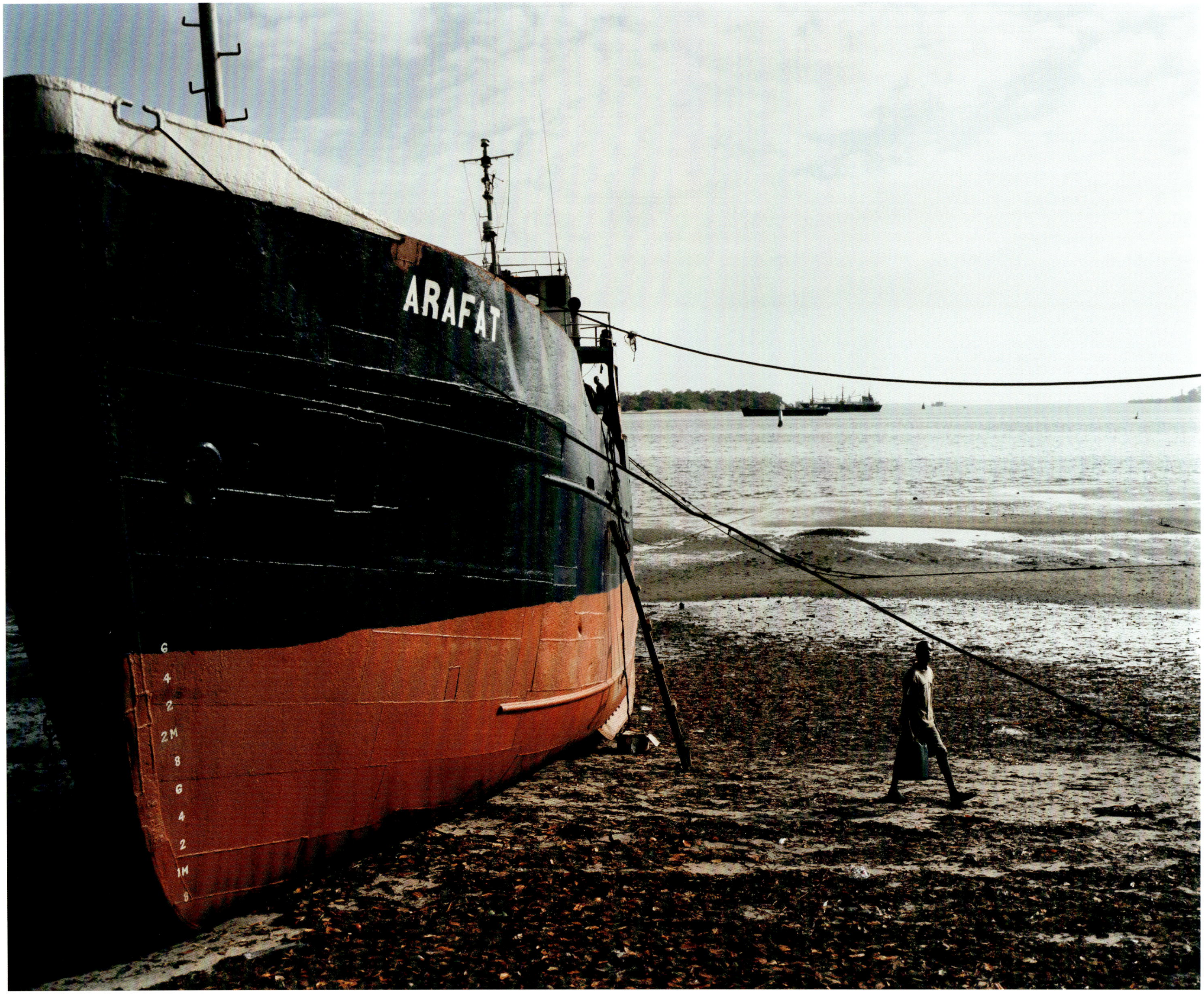

Boat needing repair sits in dry dock, Tanga, 2011

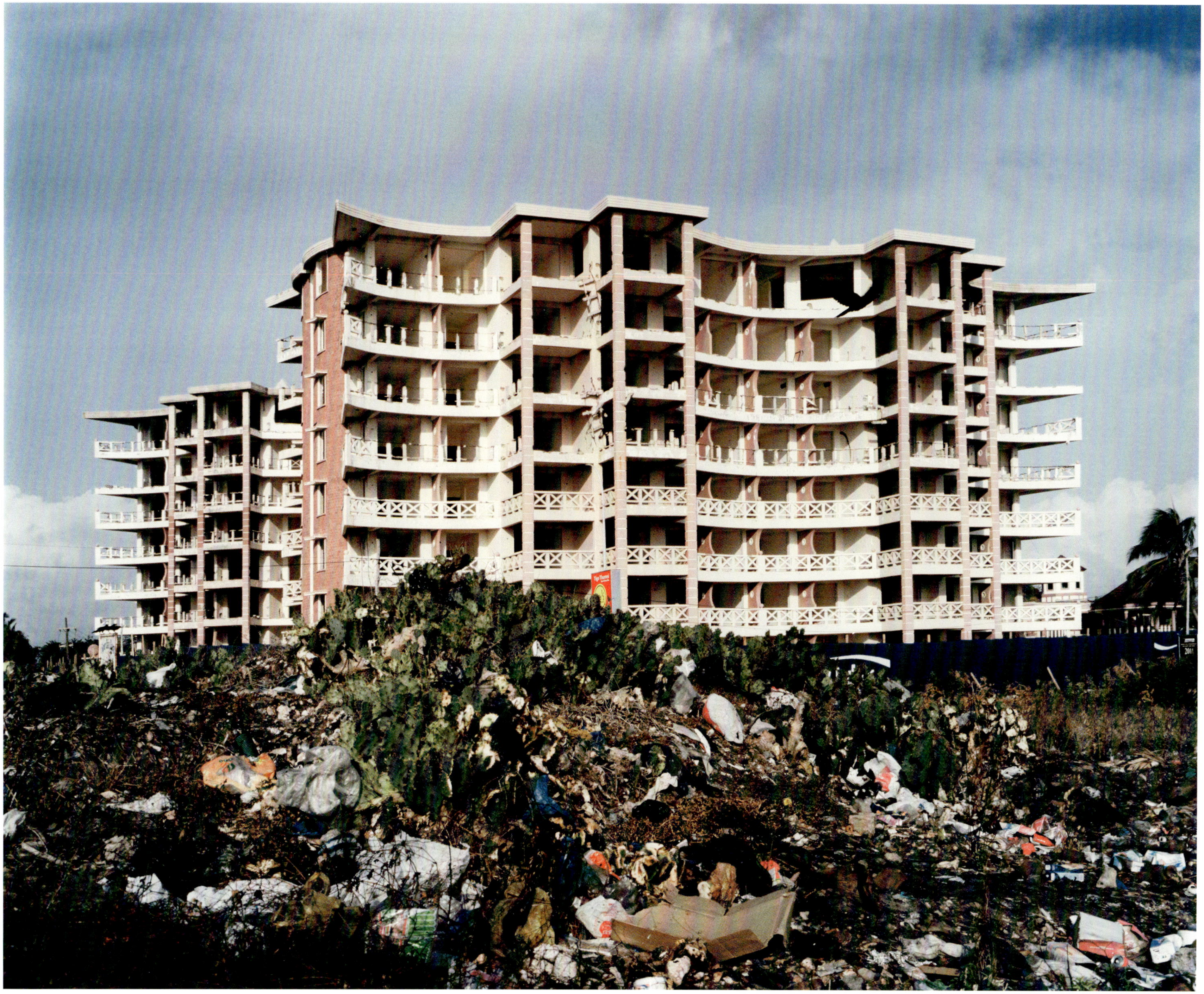

Nearly completed building stopped due to the misappropriation of funds, Masaki area, Dar es Salaam, 2012

In Tanga it felt like its former German and British colonial masters had left only the day before. Like so many places in Africa, it is a city that has been largely abandoned by the central government. Its people still have little say in their destiny; they are suspended between a colonial past and an uncertain future. I wanted to photograph the town because it was so easy to imagine what it must have been like to live there in days gone by. Exploring the streets and alleys of this sleepy town was like walking across the pages of a history book.

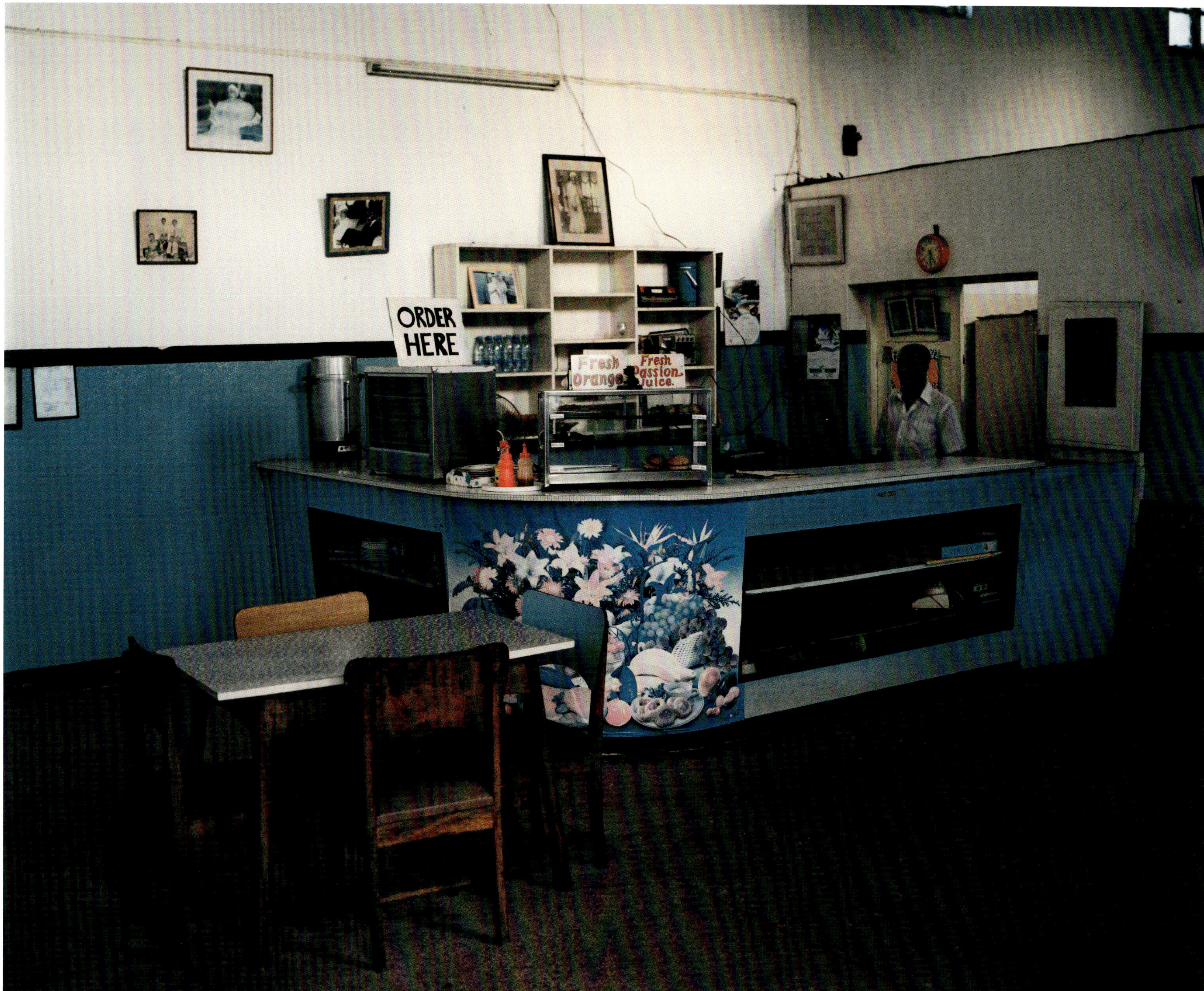
ORDER
HERE
Fresh
Orange
Fresh
Passion
Juice

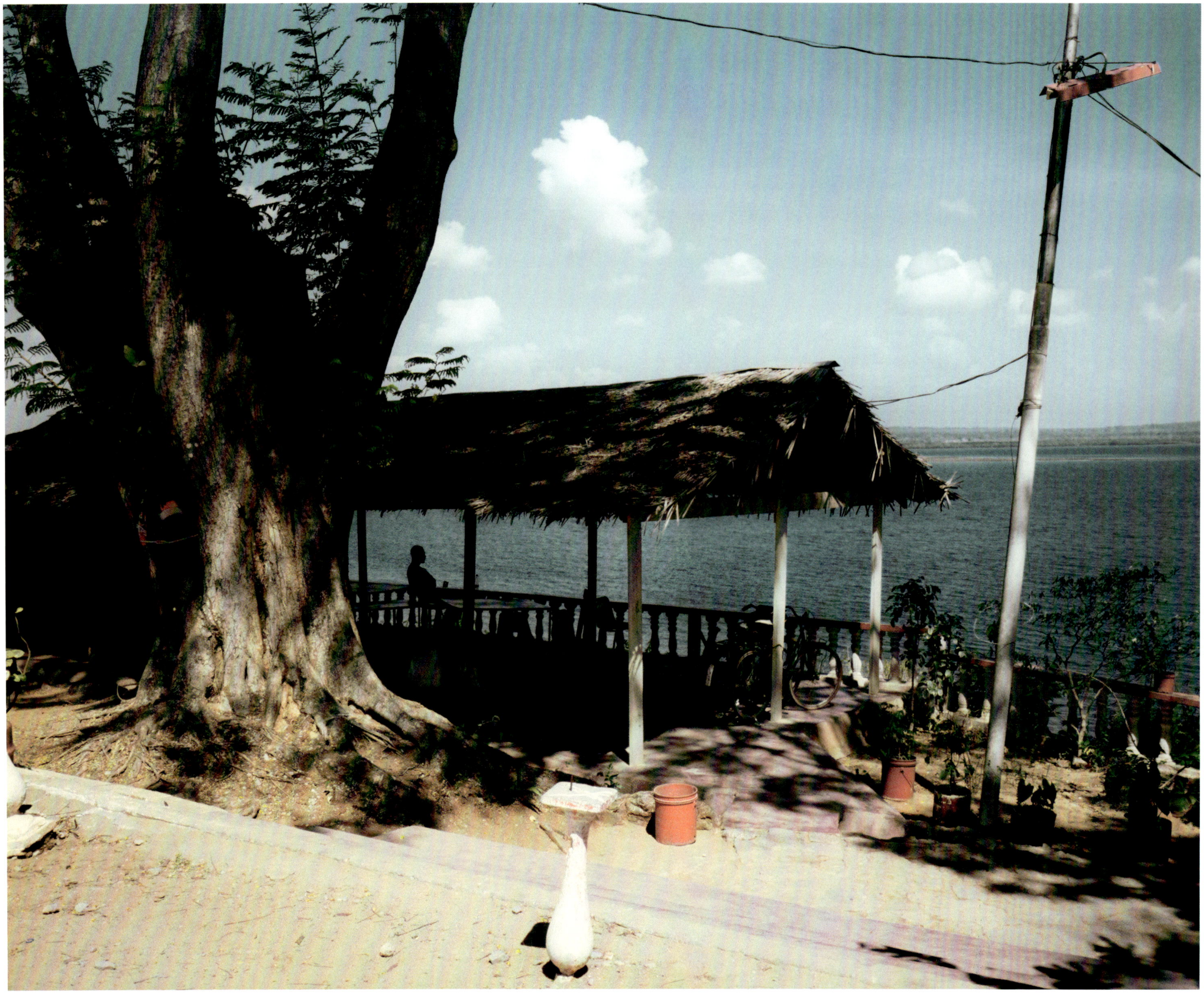

Near Tanga Yacht Club, 2011

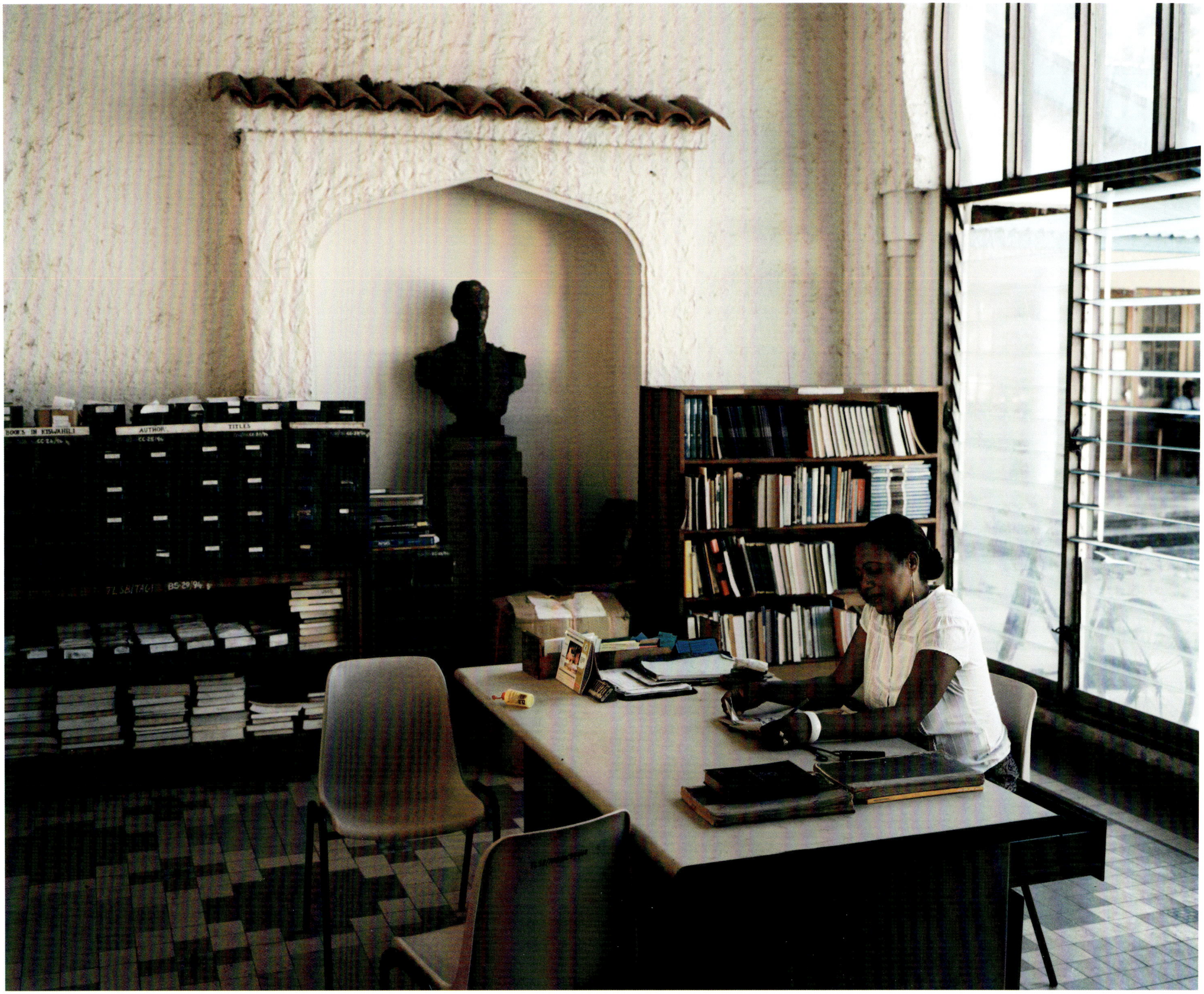

Tanga public library with a bust of King George VI, 2011

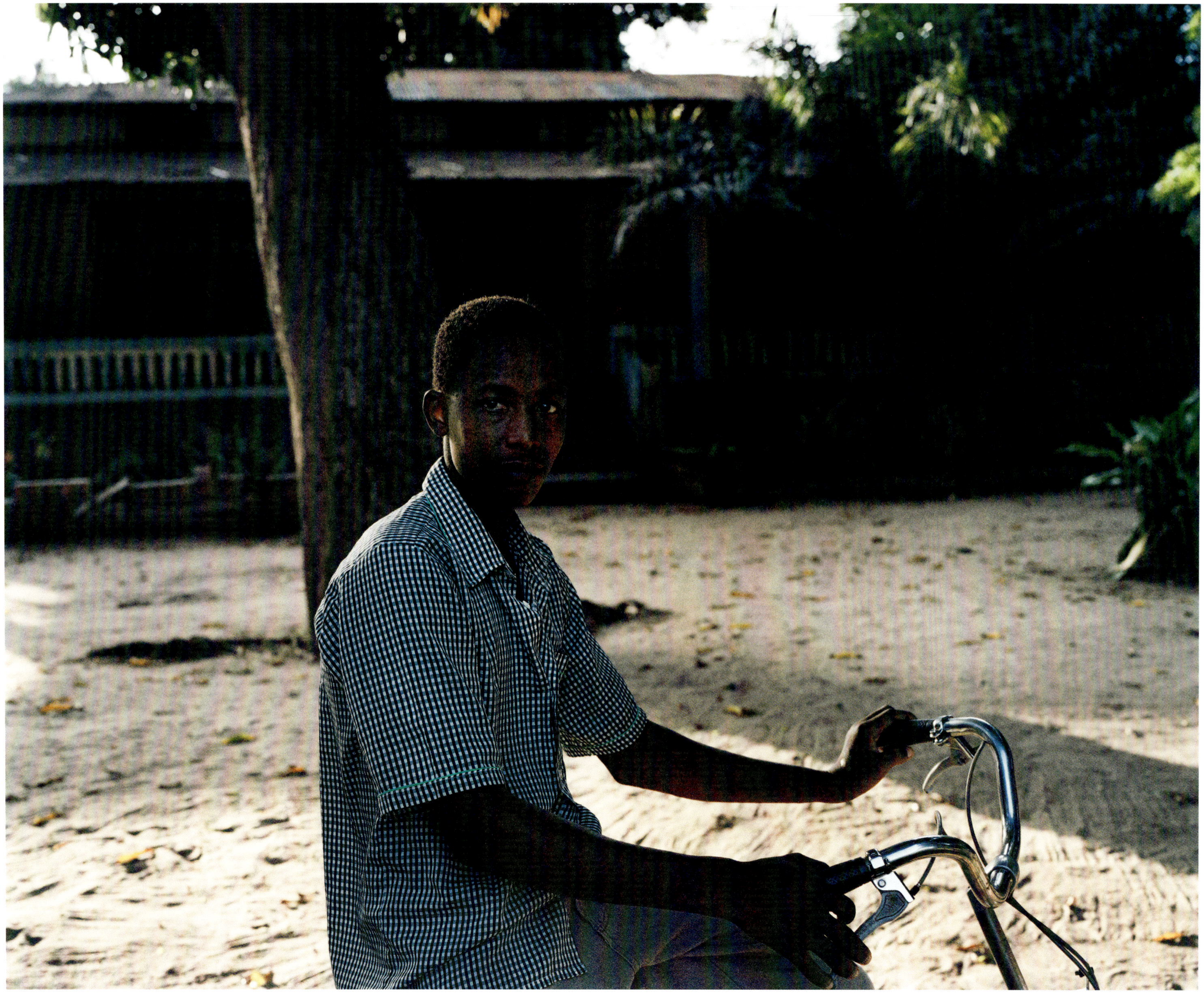

Near the District Commissioner's Office, Pangani, 2011

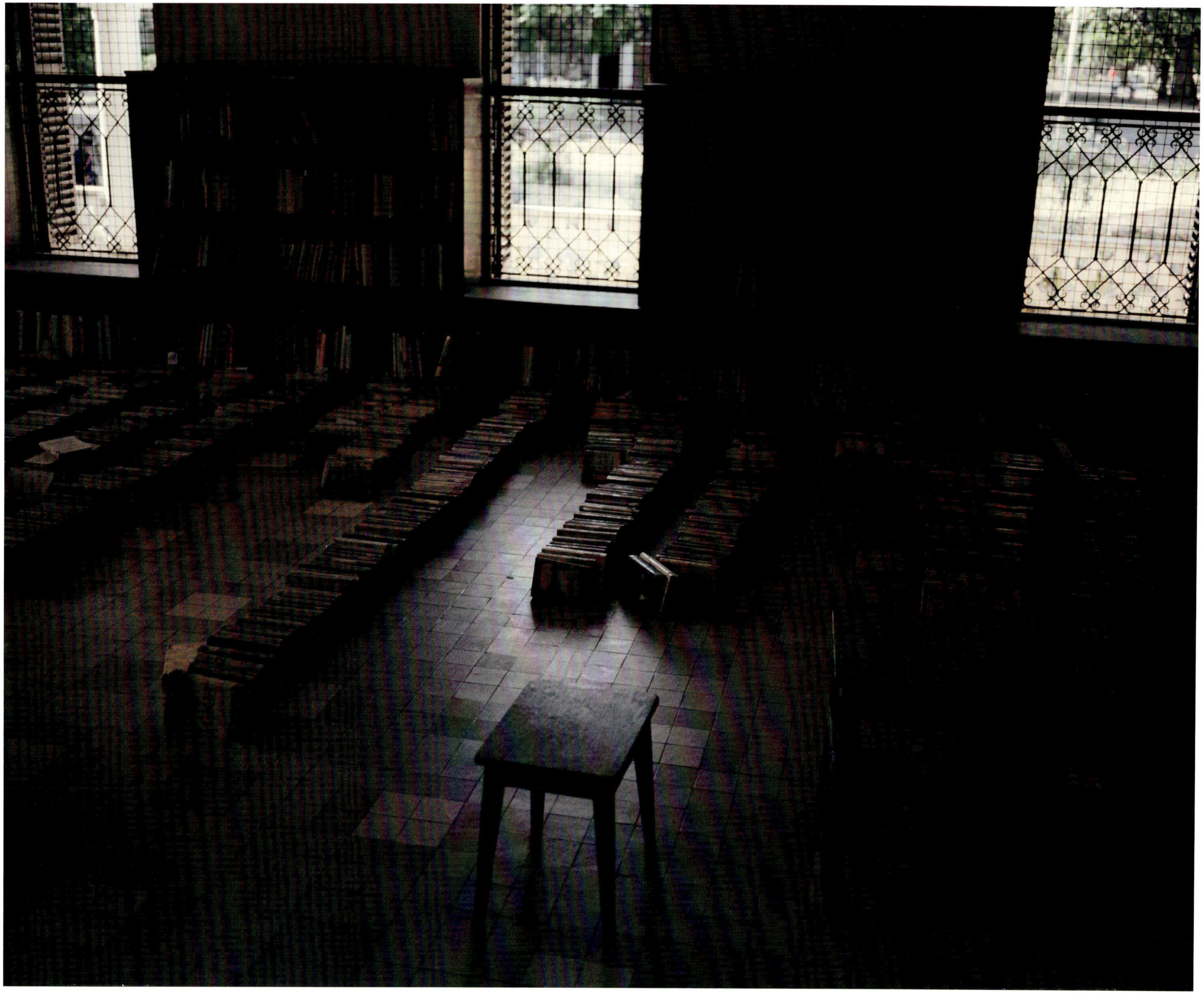

Tanga public library, 2011

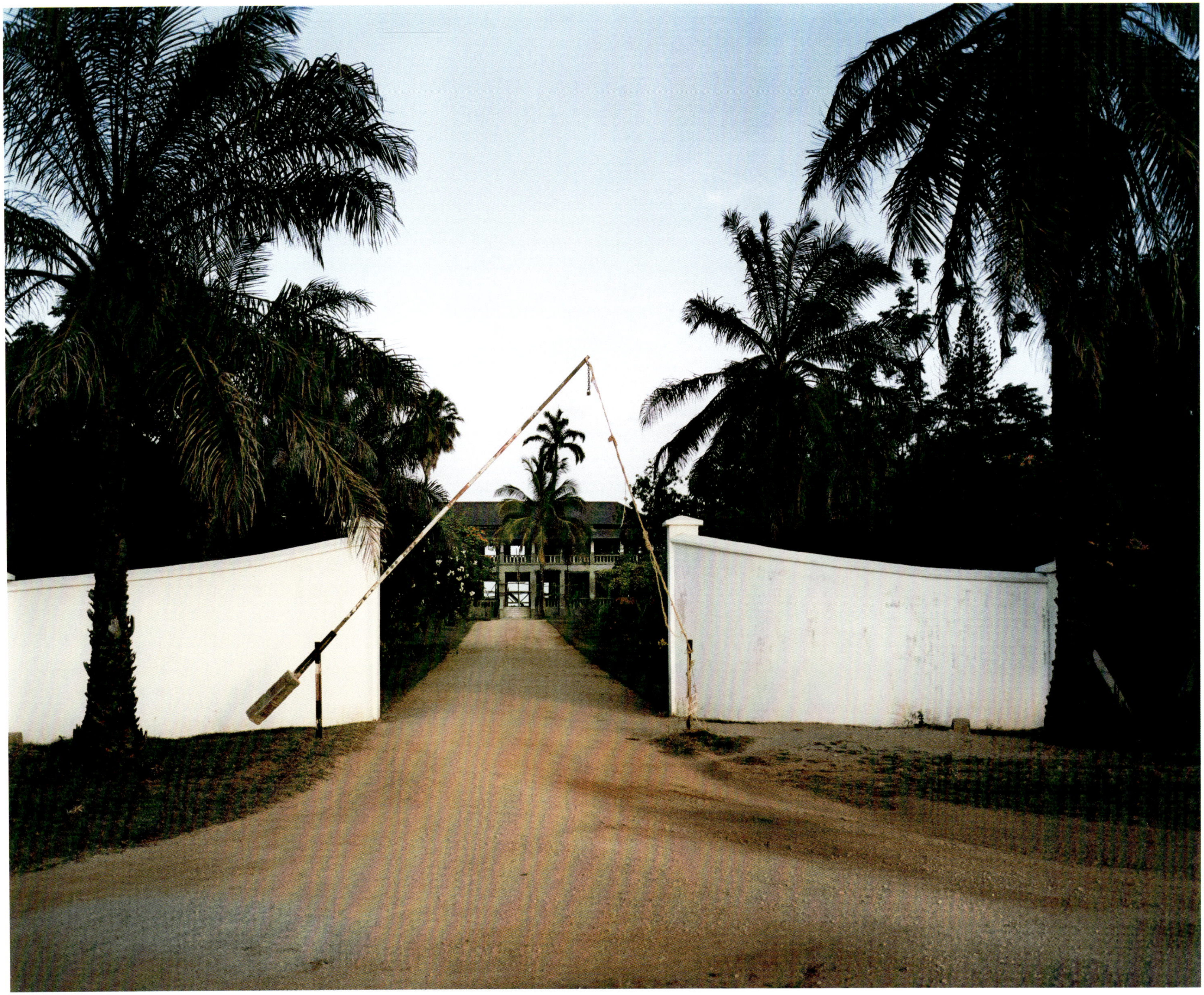

Private residence along the Pangani coastline, 2011

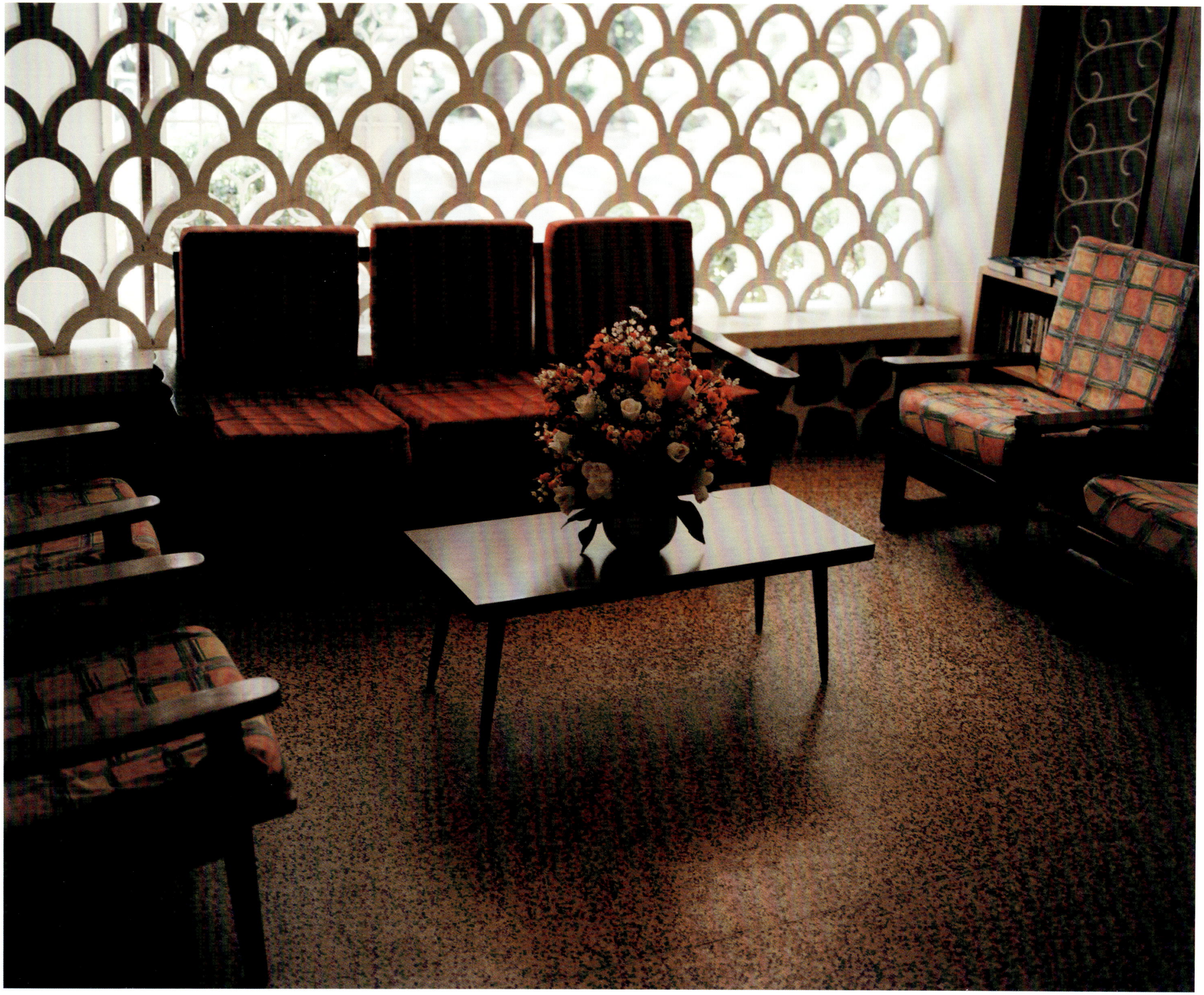

Hotel lobby, Tanga, 2011

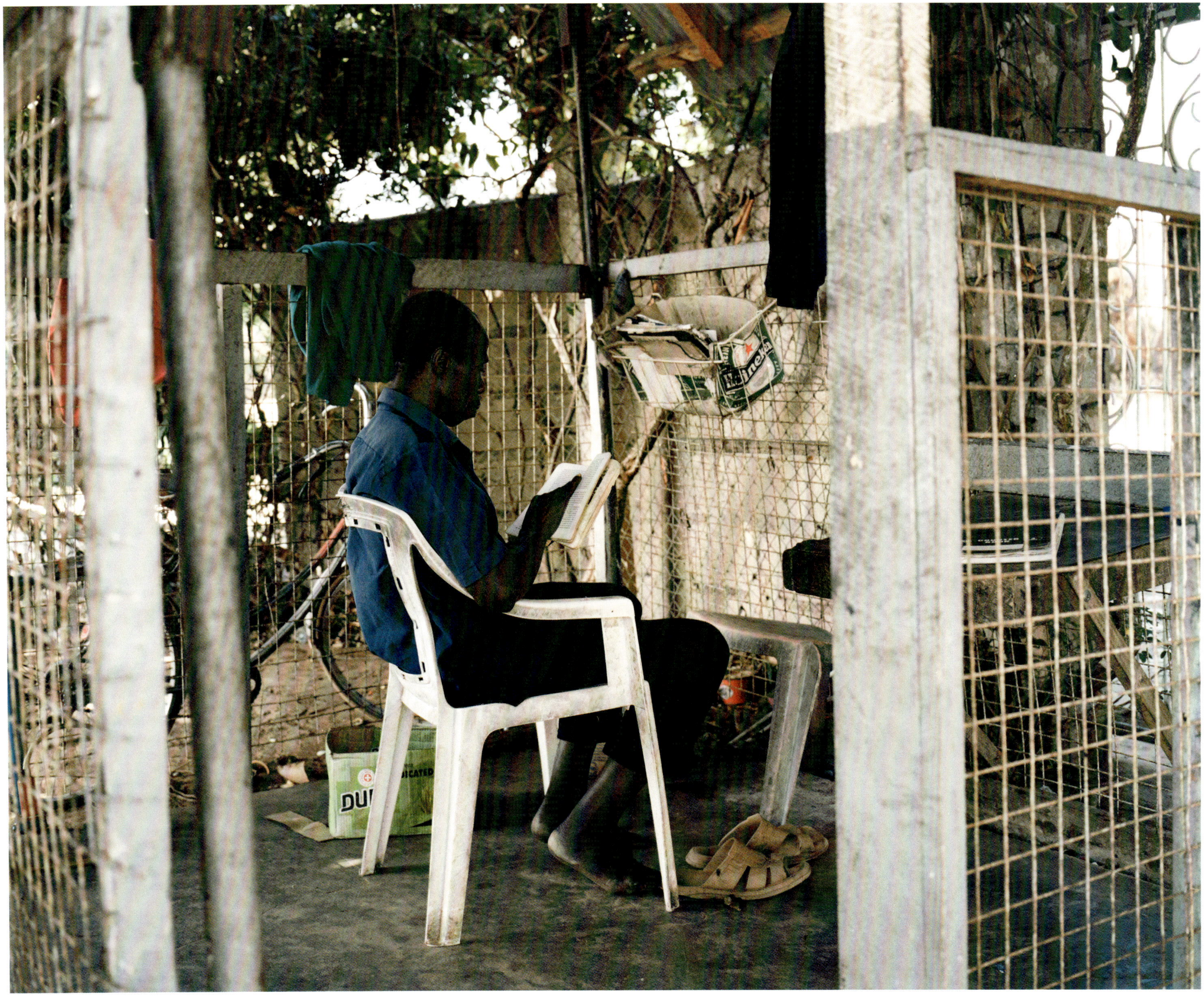

Security guard reading his book, Tanga, 2011

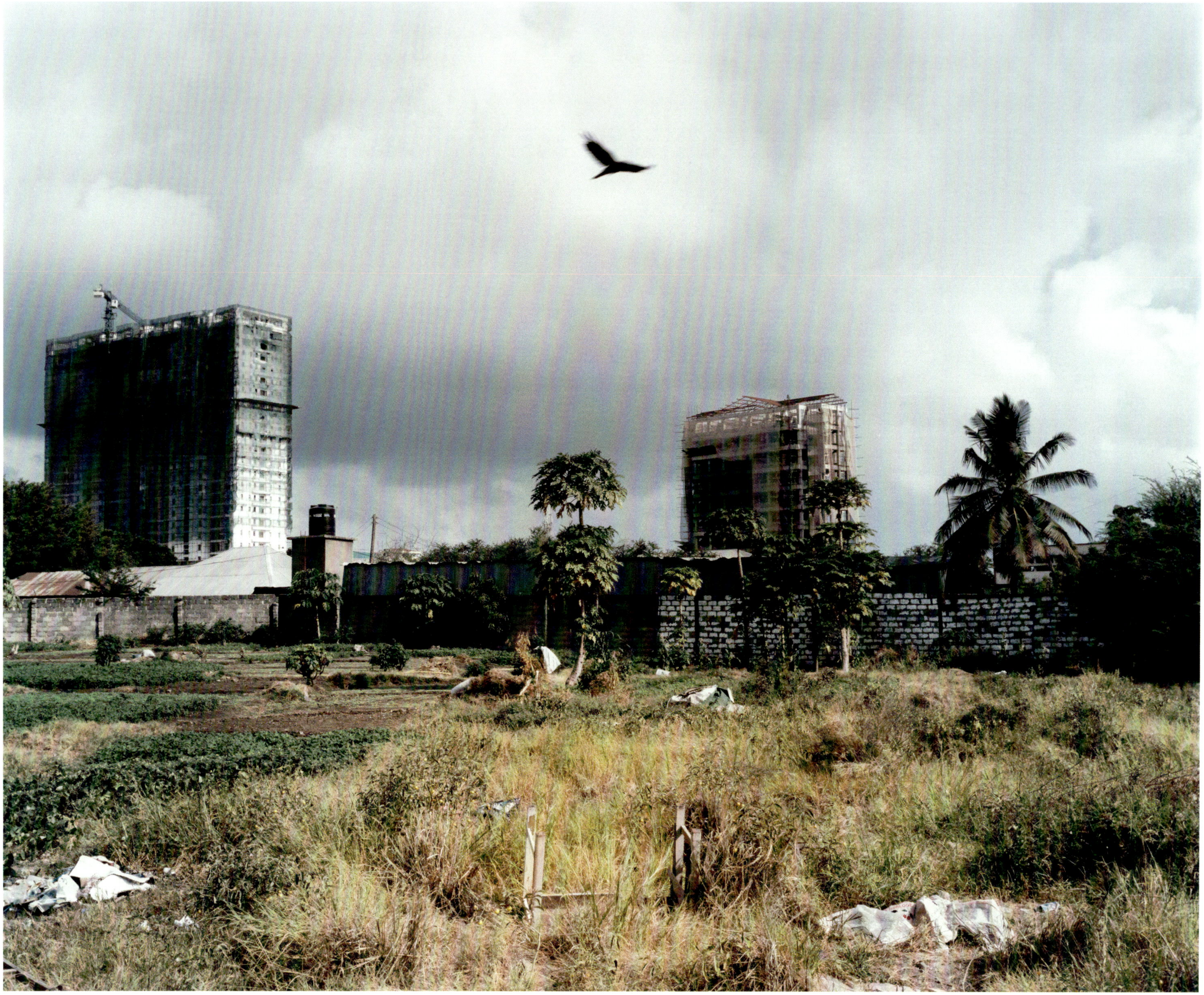

Buildings under construction, Dar es Salaam, 2011

Fisherman near the town of Pangani, 2011

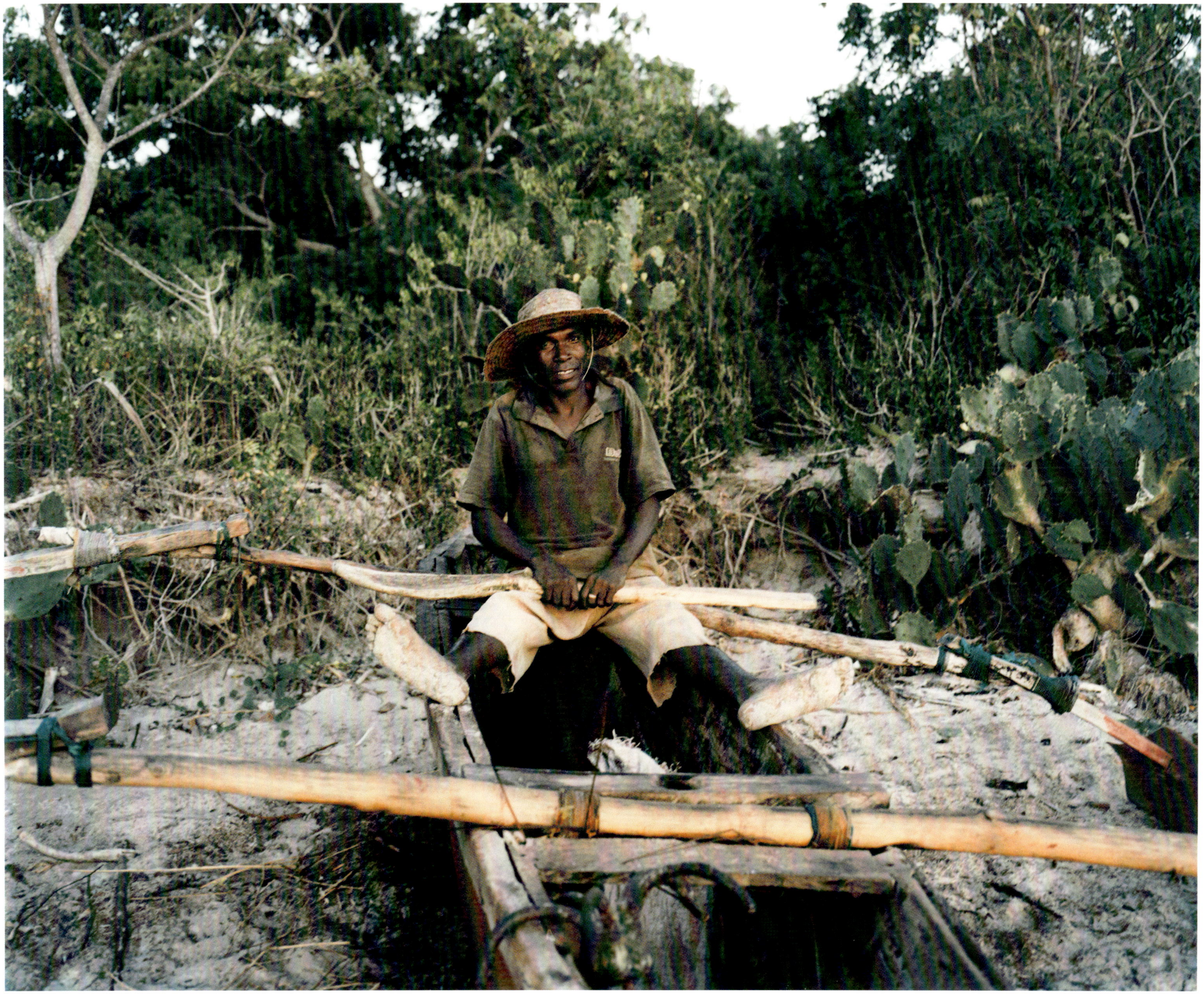

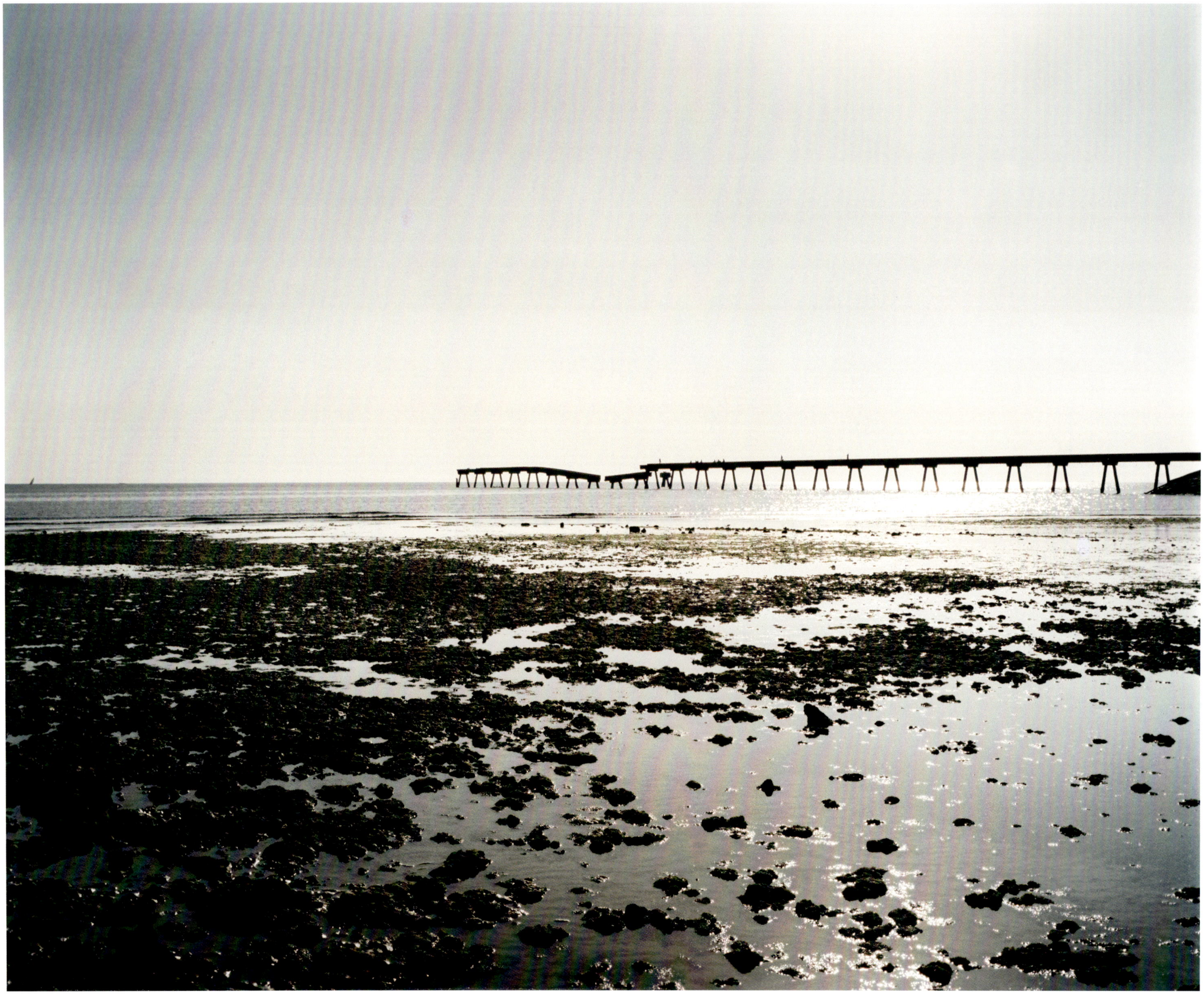

Broken pier, Ocean Drive, Tanga, 2011

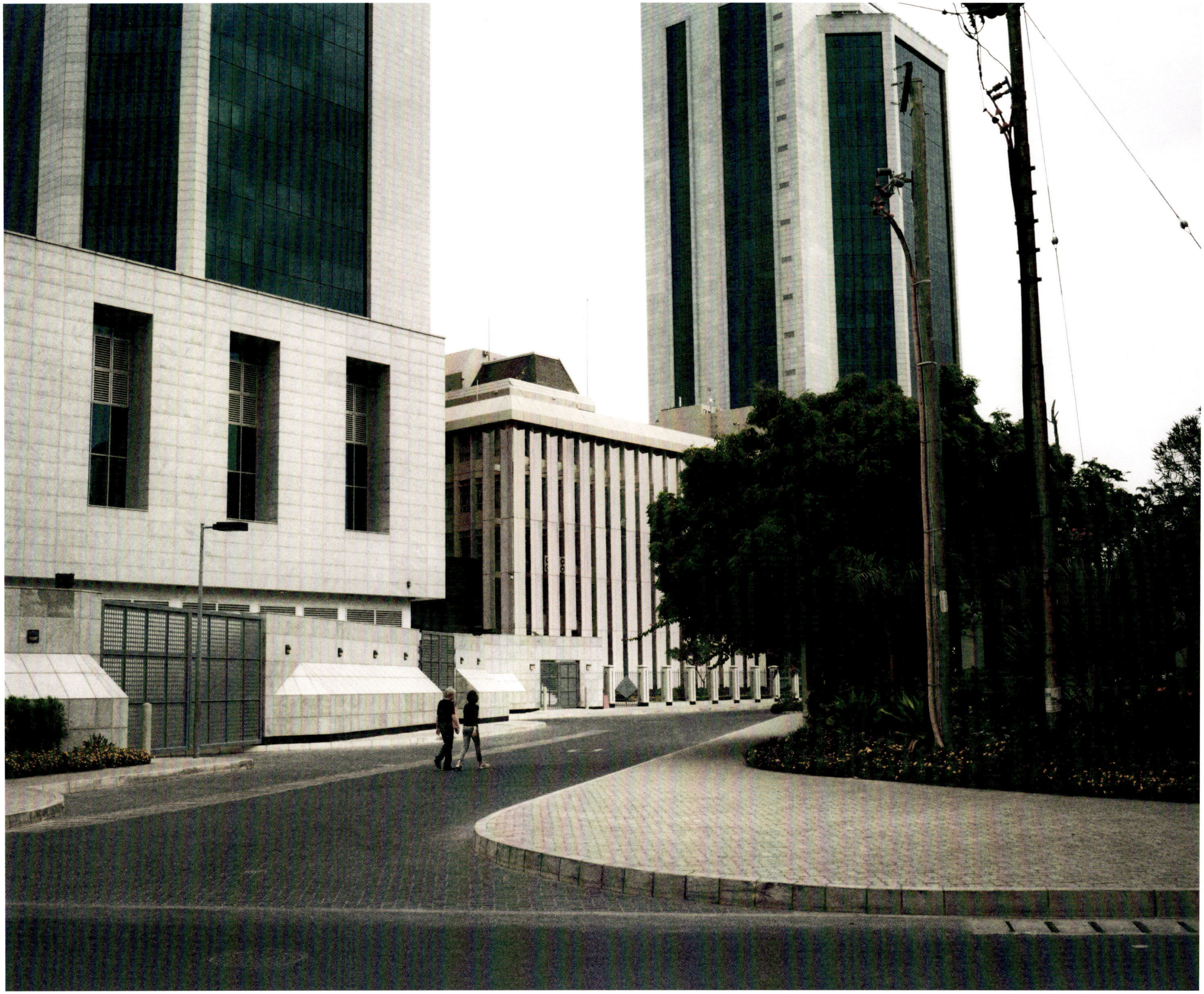

Business district, Dar es Salaam, 2011

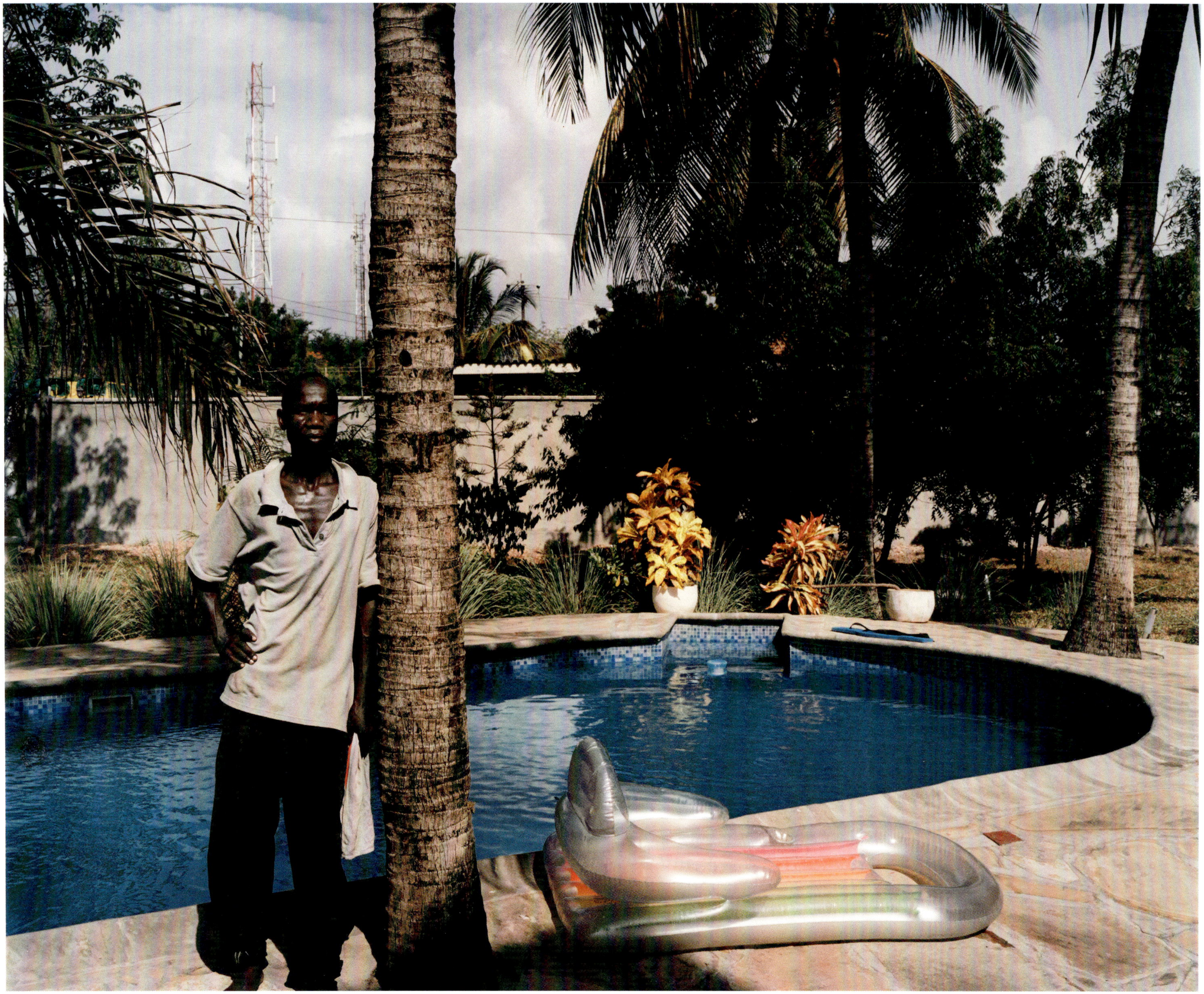

Gardener, private residence, Dar es Salaam, 2011

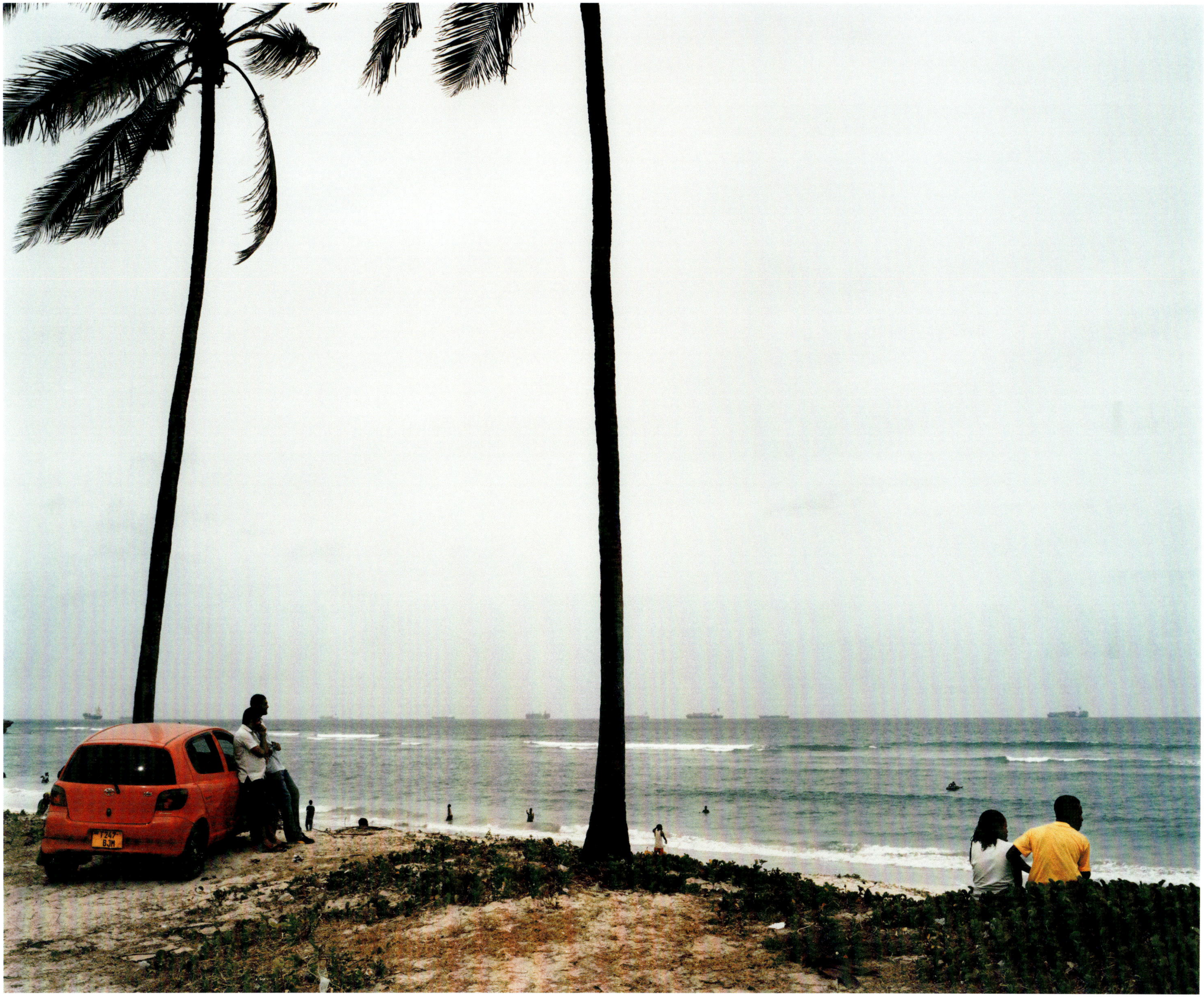

Public beach, Masaki area, Dar es Salaam, 2011

Fisherman leaving the shores of Pangani for the day, 2011

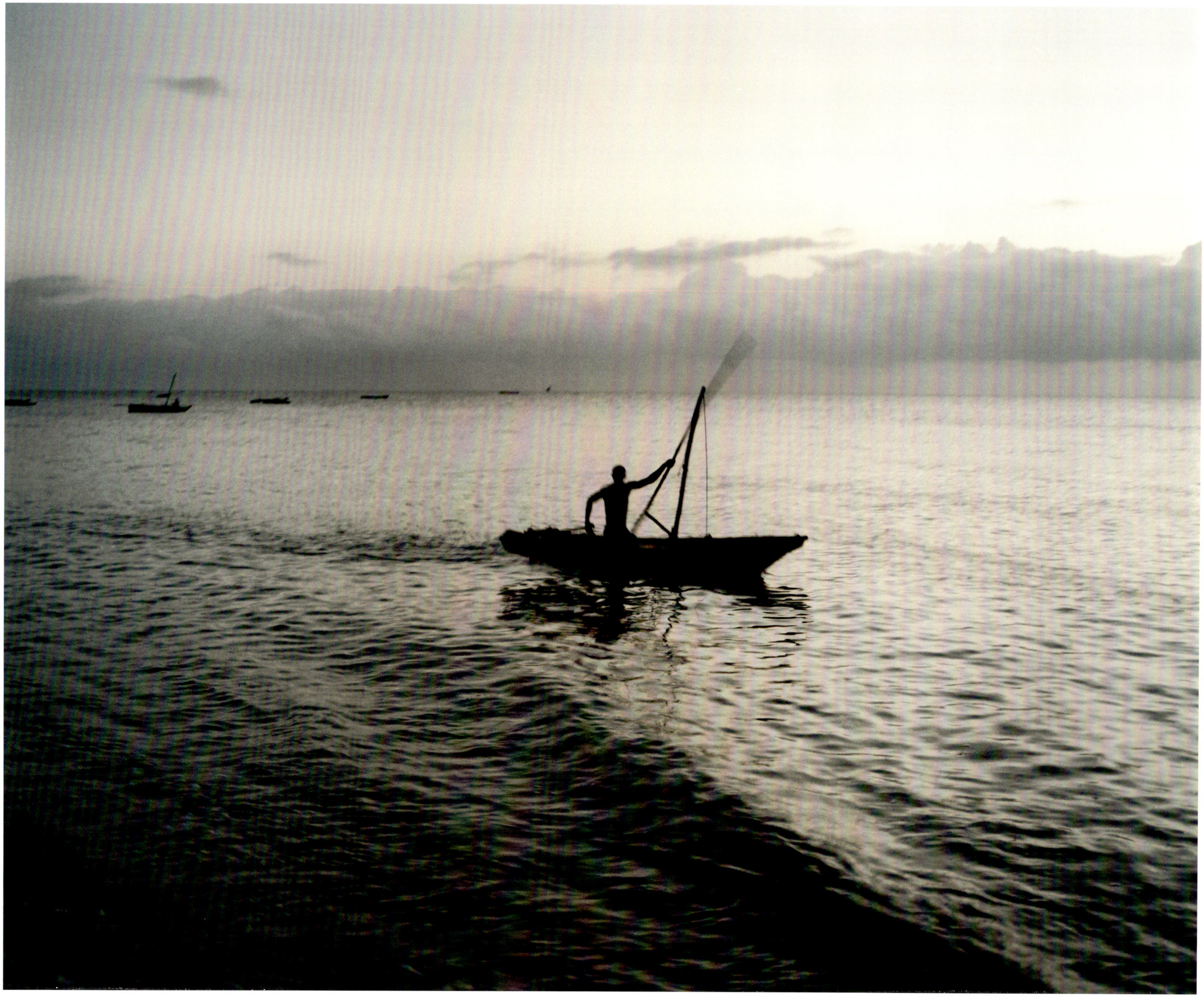

KENYA

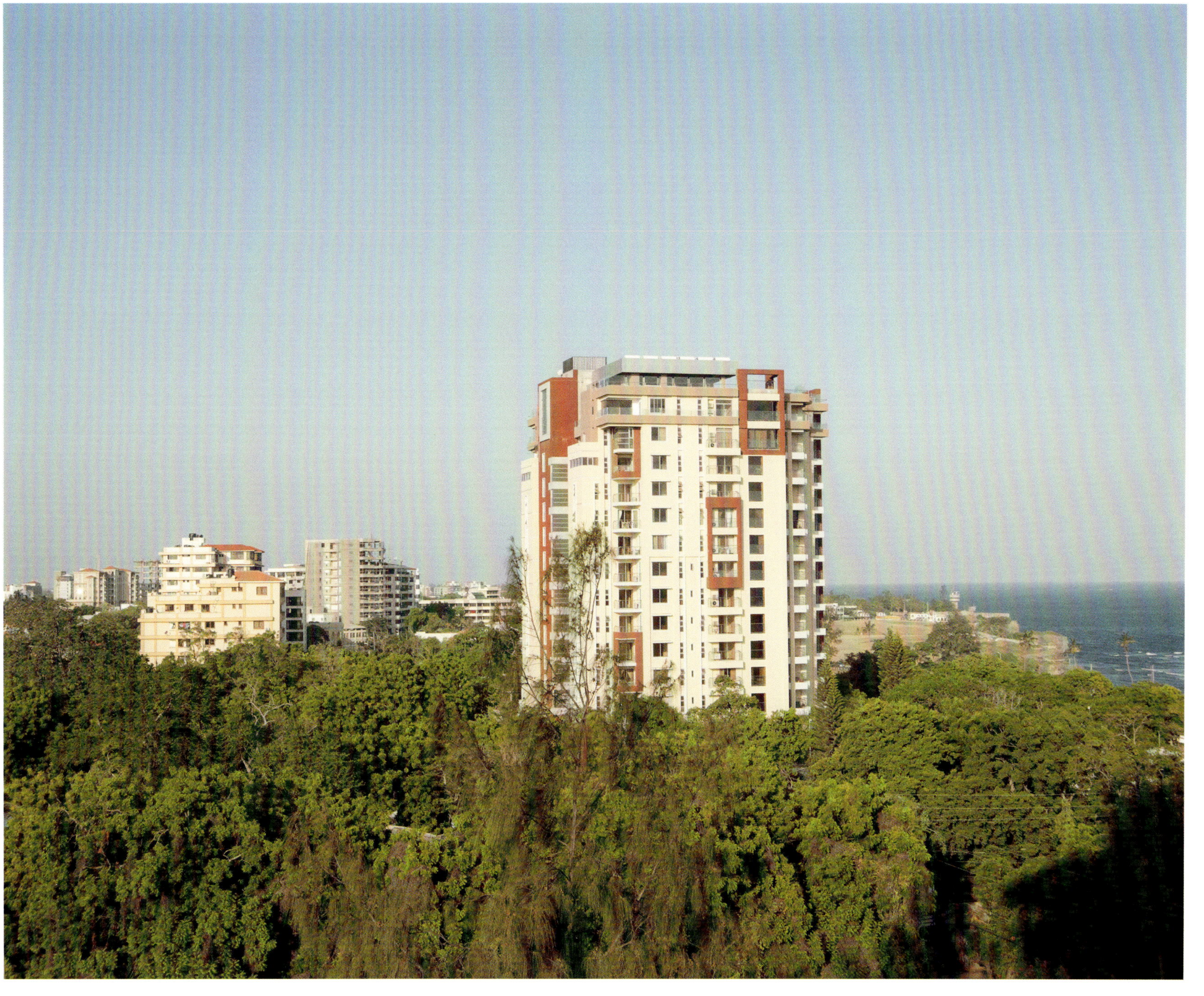

Mombasa Island, 2014

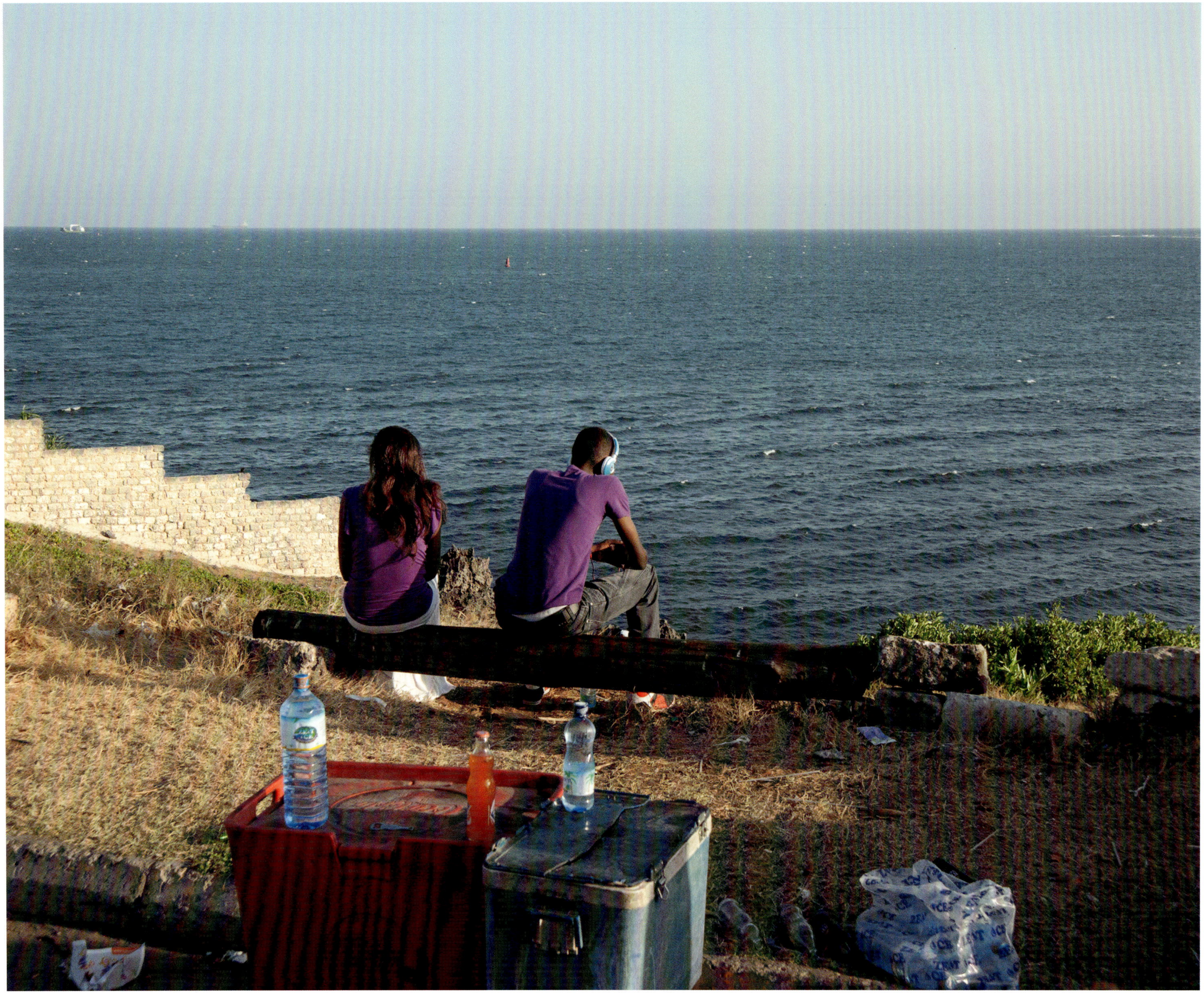

Mama Ngina Drive, Mombasa Island, 2014

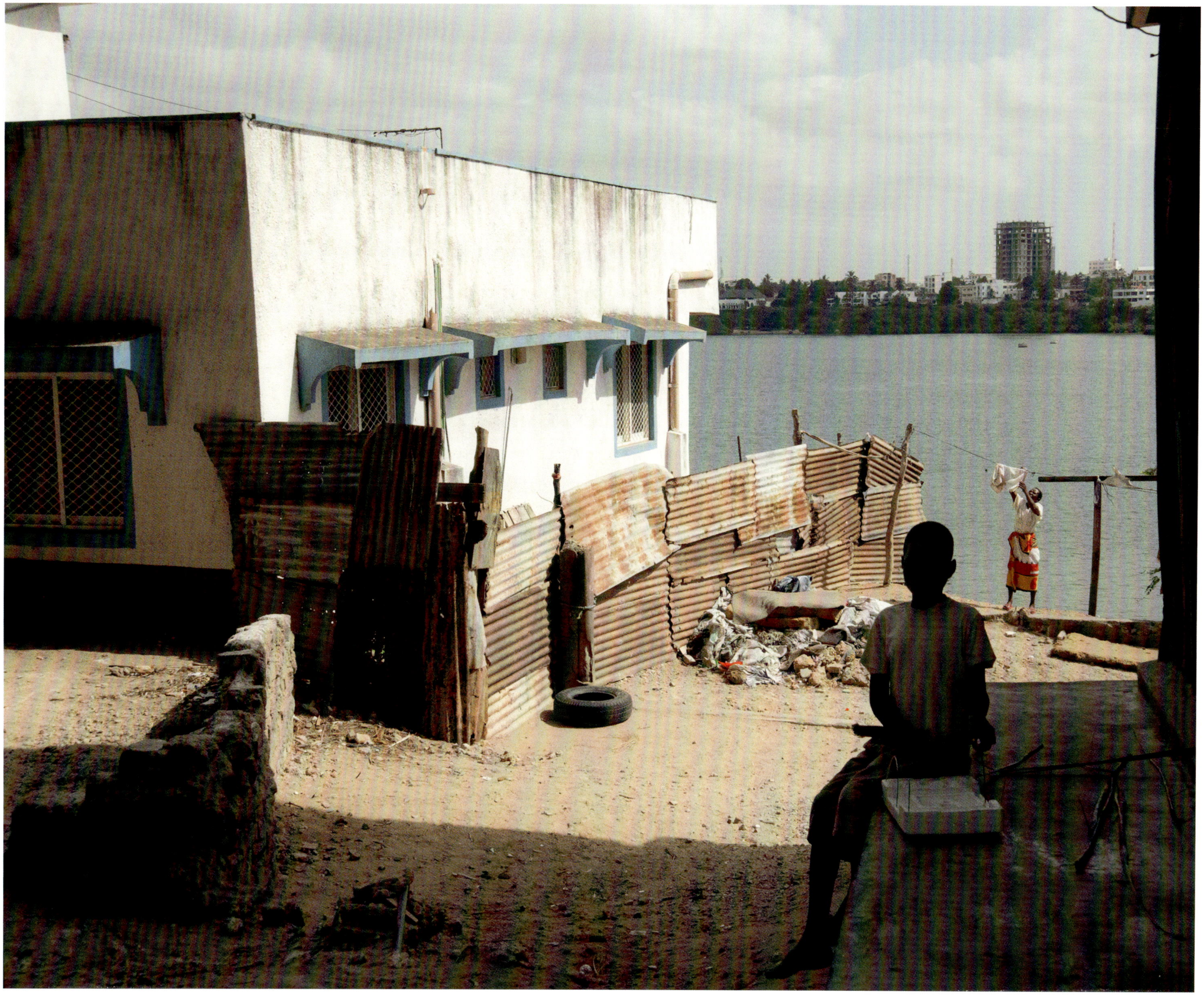

Old town, Mombasa Island, 2014

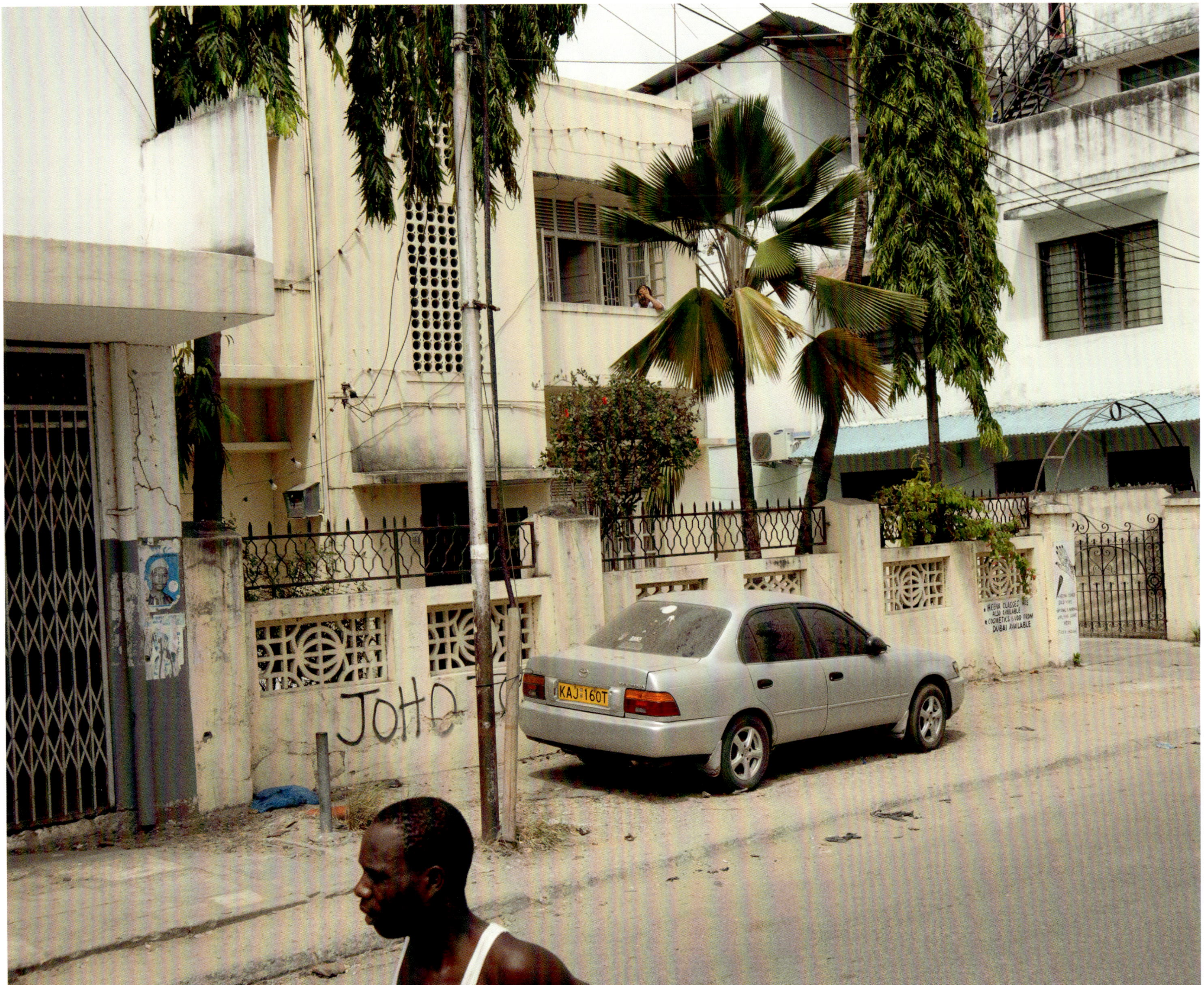

Ganjoni area, Mombasa Island, 2014

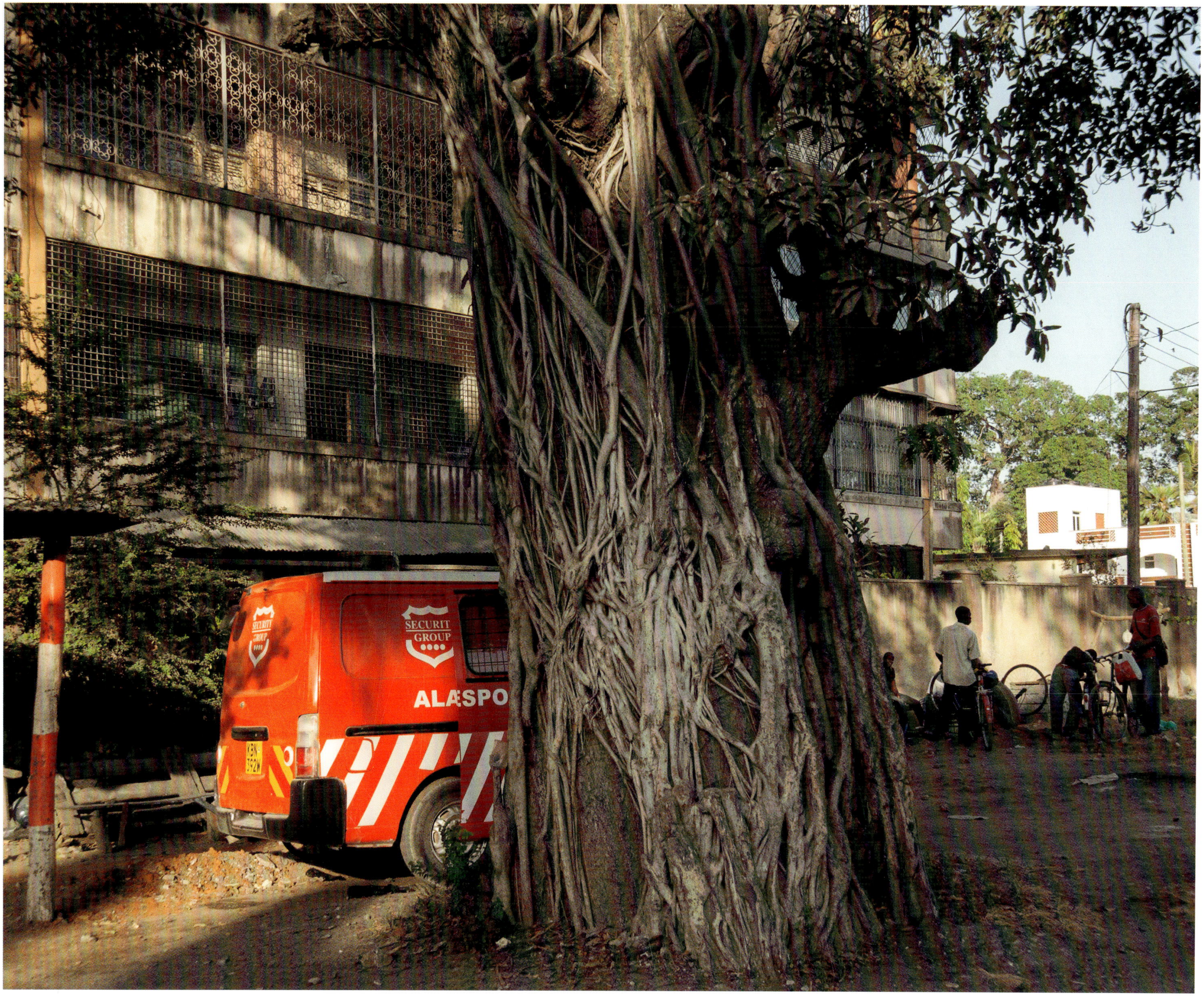

Private security van, Mombasa Island, 2014

Lamu is a tiny island located off Kenya's northern coast. At the end of the nineties, it had the questionable good fortune to become a jet-set destination: sun, beach, and an exotic culture. Its popularity lasted not much more than a decade before lawlessness in neighboring Somalia spilled over the border. Tourists were kidnapped on two separate occasions. In one of the incidents, a man was shot and killed. The international community issued travel warnings, and it wasn't long before Lamu had reverted to its old self—a tranquil Swahili town on the edge of the Indian Ocean. I have been going to Lamu since I was sixteen years old. Nothing much has changed. It is still a place of tropical palms and pristine, pale beaches with an overlay of Arab tradition. Lamu may be a tranquil oasis sandwiched between the blue of sky and ocean, but the story is different elsewhere in Kenya. It is the story of corruption and violence. The rich and the poor abuse the rule of law equally. Crime has become the means of survival for millions of jobless and disenfranchised Kenyans. The elite is so mired in corruption that they have become disconnected from reality, no longer seeing or caring about the suffering of their fellow countrymen. One man's economic boom, another's destitution: Kenya's real-estate sector saw a sharp rise in 2012 that benefited those who were already rich. Nairobi and Mombasa were the only cities in the southern hemisphere to have reported double-digit property price increases.

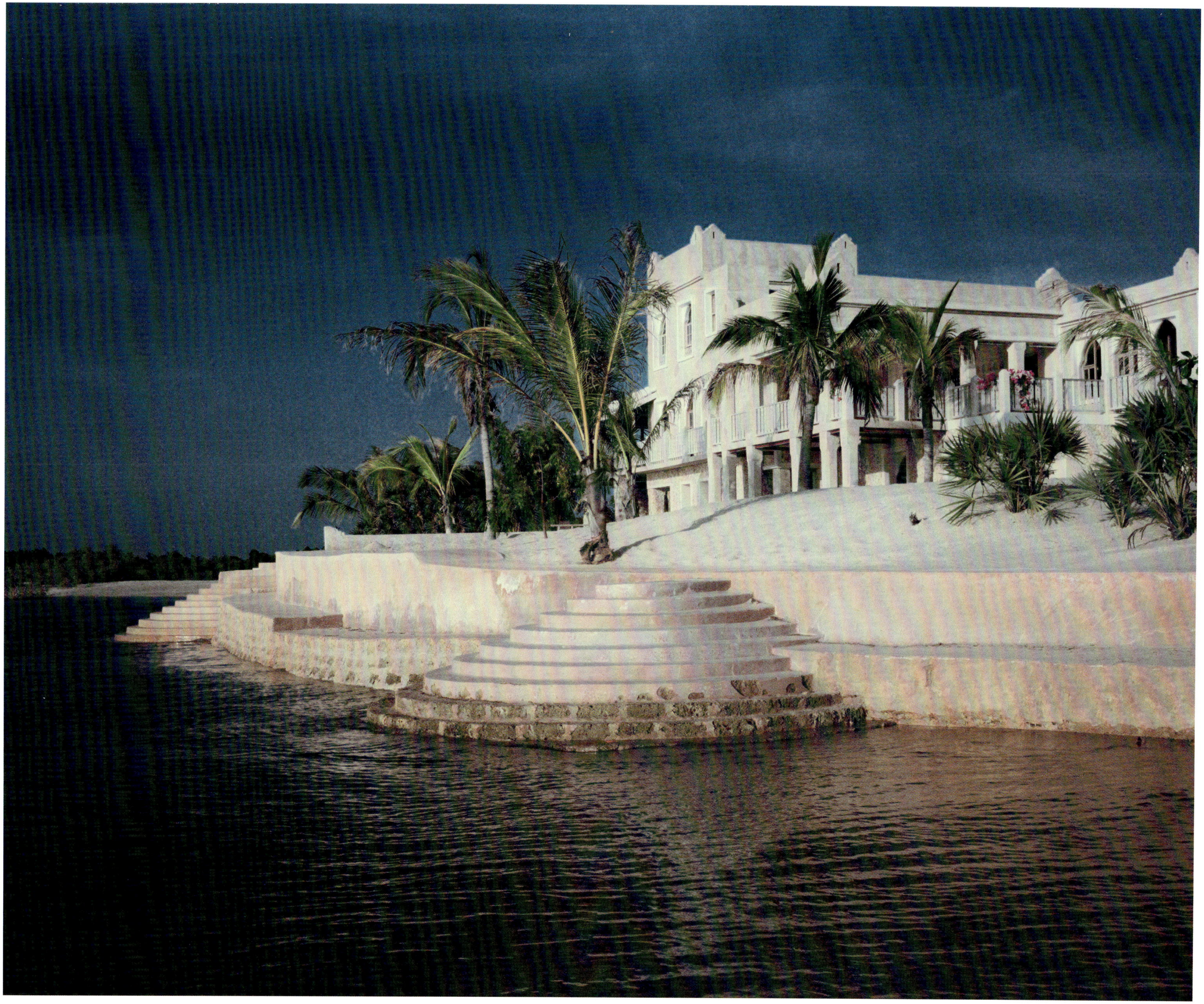

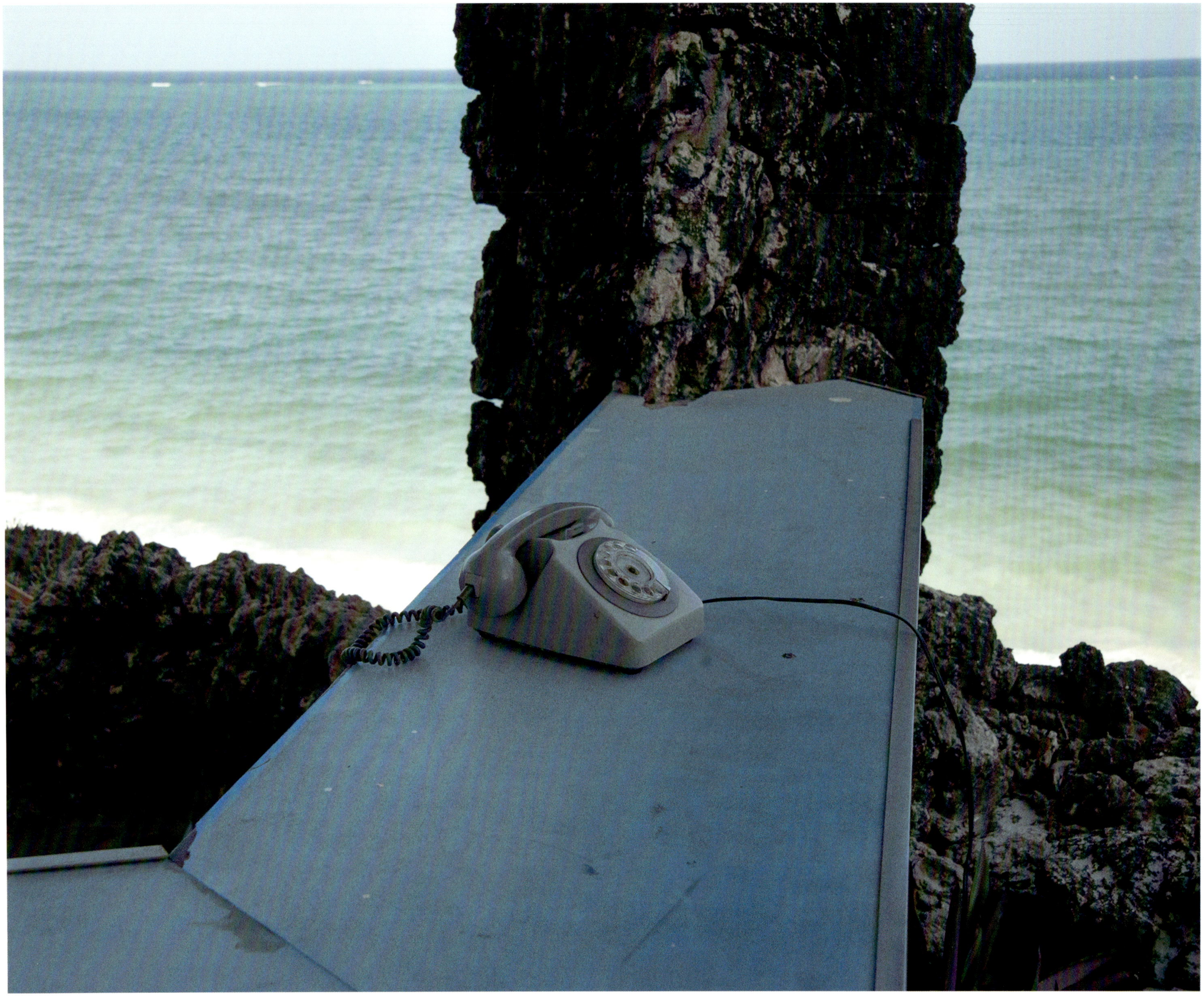

An old telephone still in use, Nyali area, Mombasa, 2014

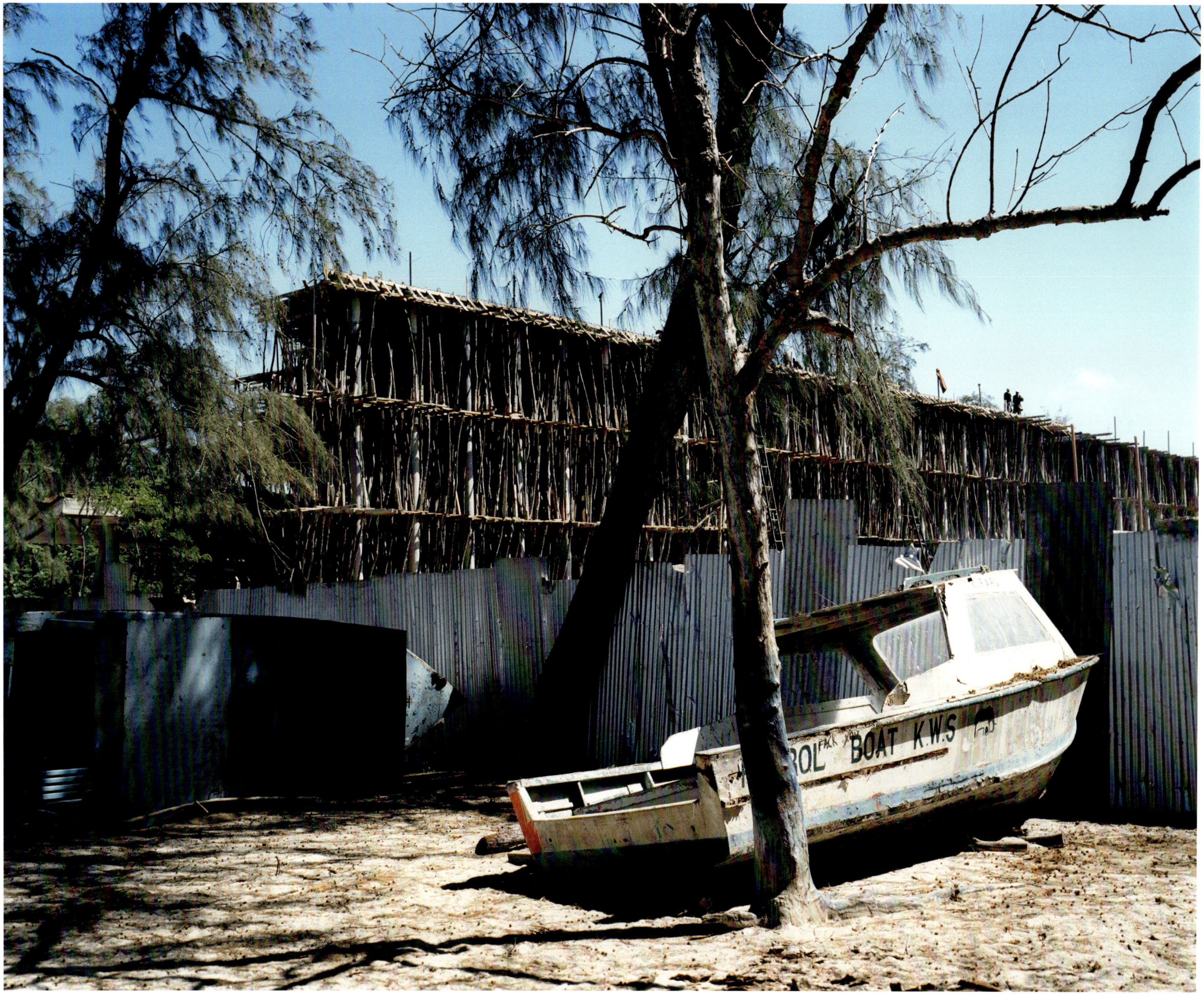

Hotel under construction, Malindi, 2014

Hotel, Nyali area, Mombasa, 2014

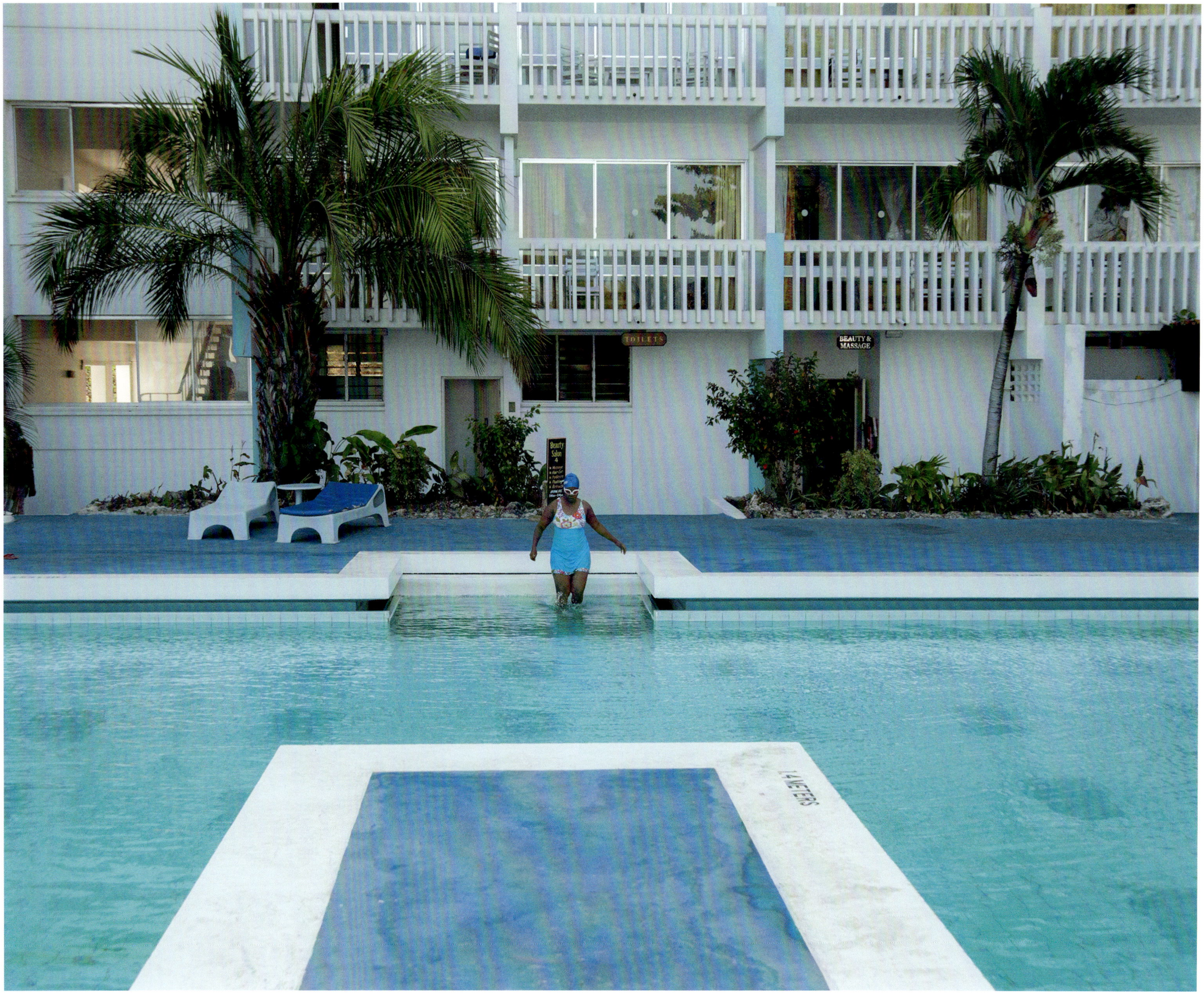
TOILETS
BEAUTY & MASSAGE
14 METERS

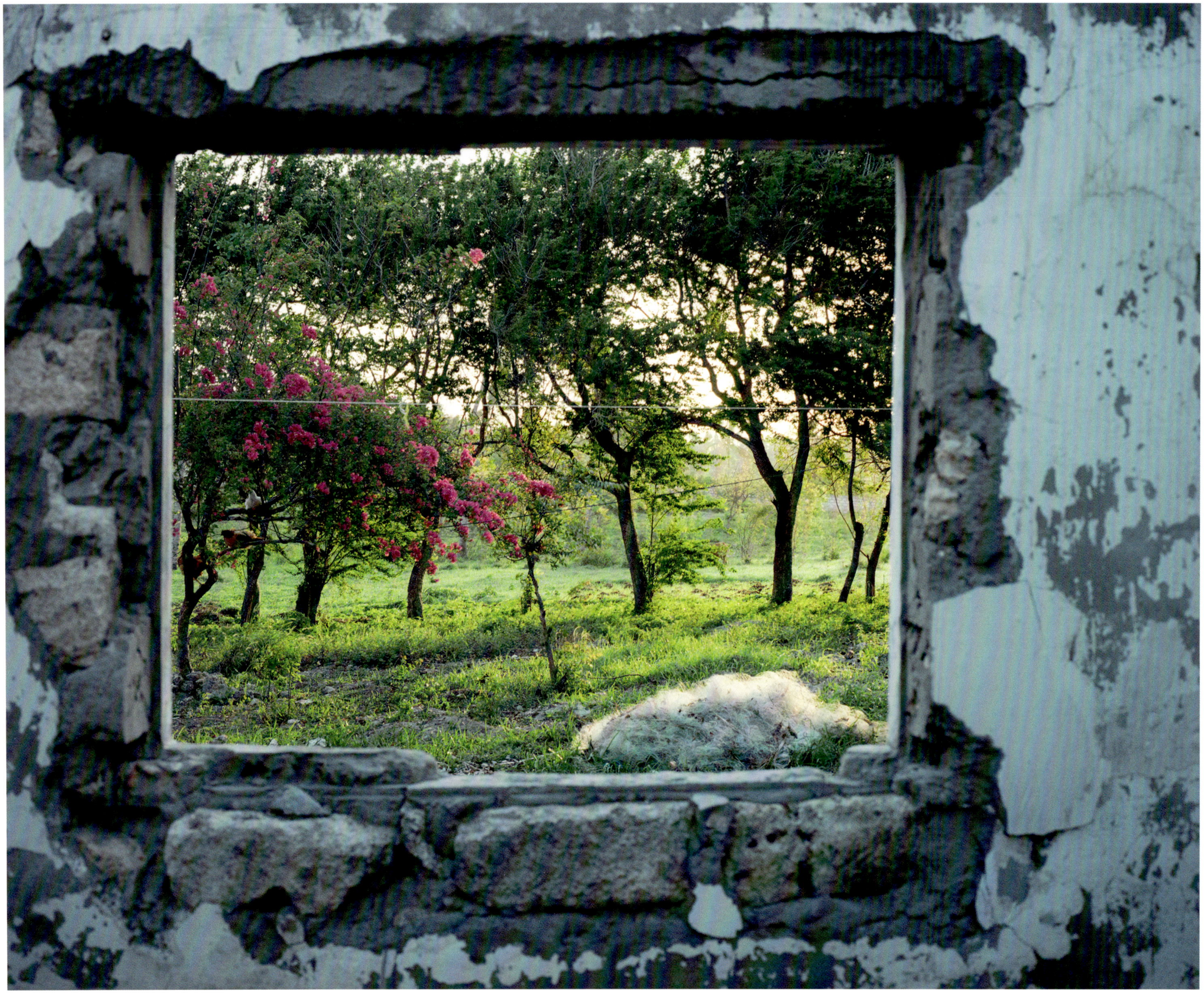

Kenyan coast, near Watamu, 2014

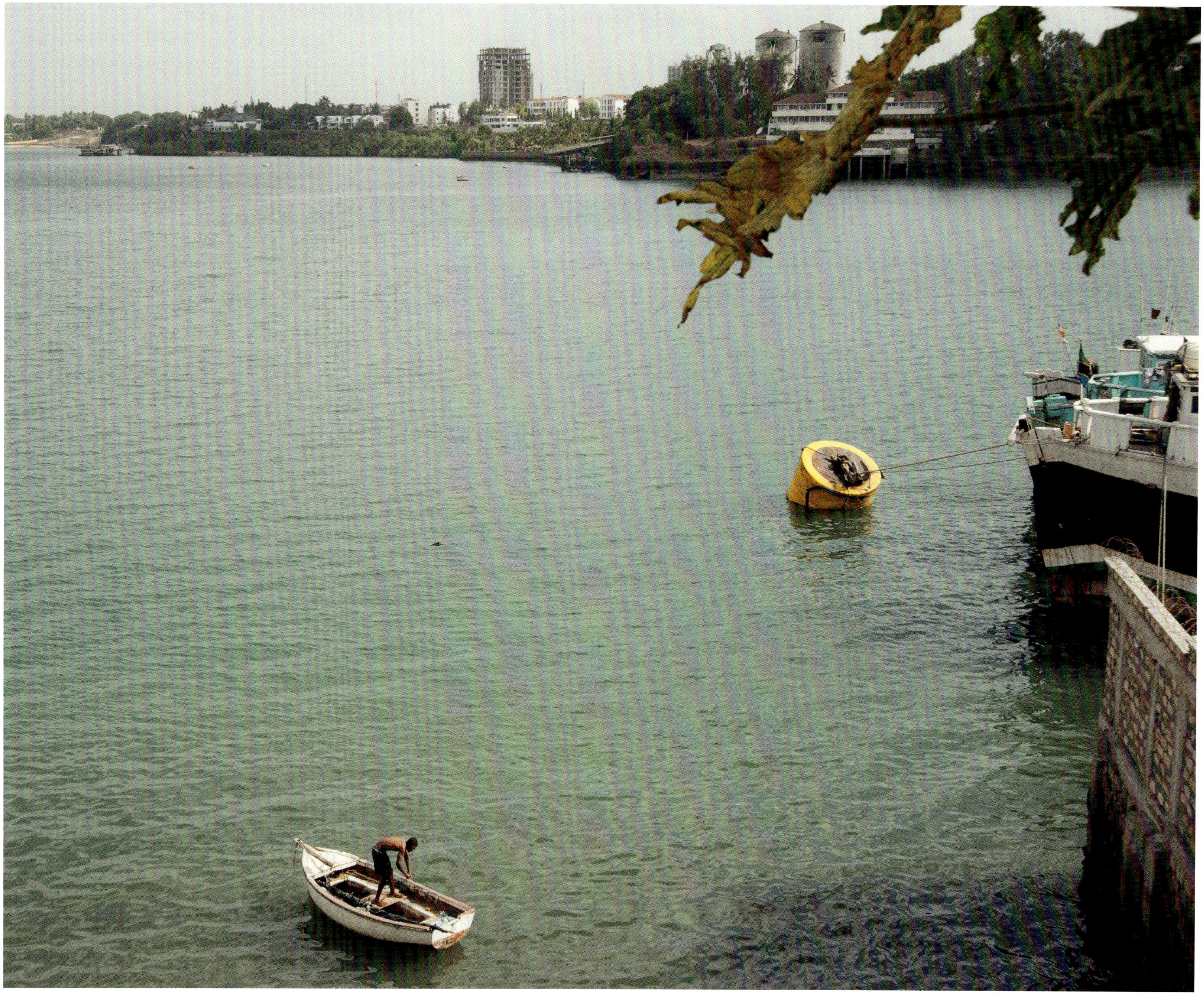

Fisherman, Mombasa Island, 2014

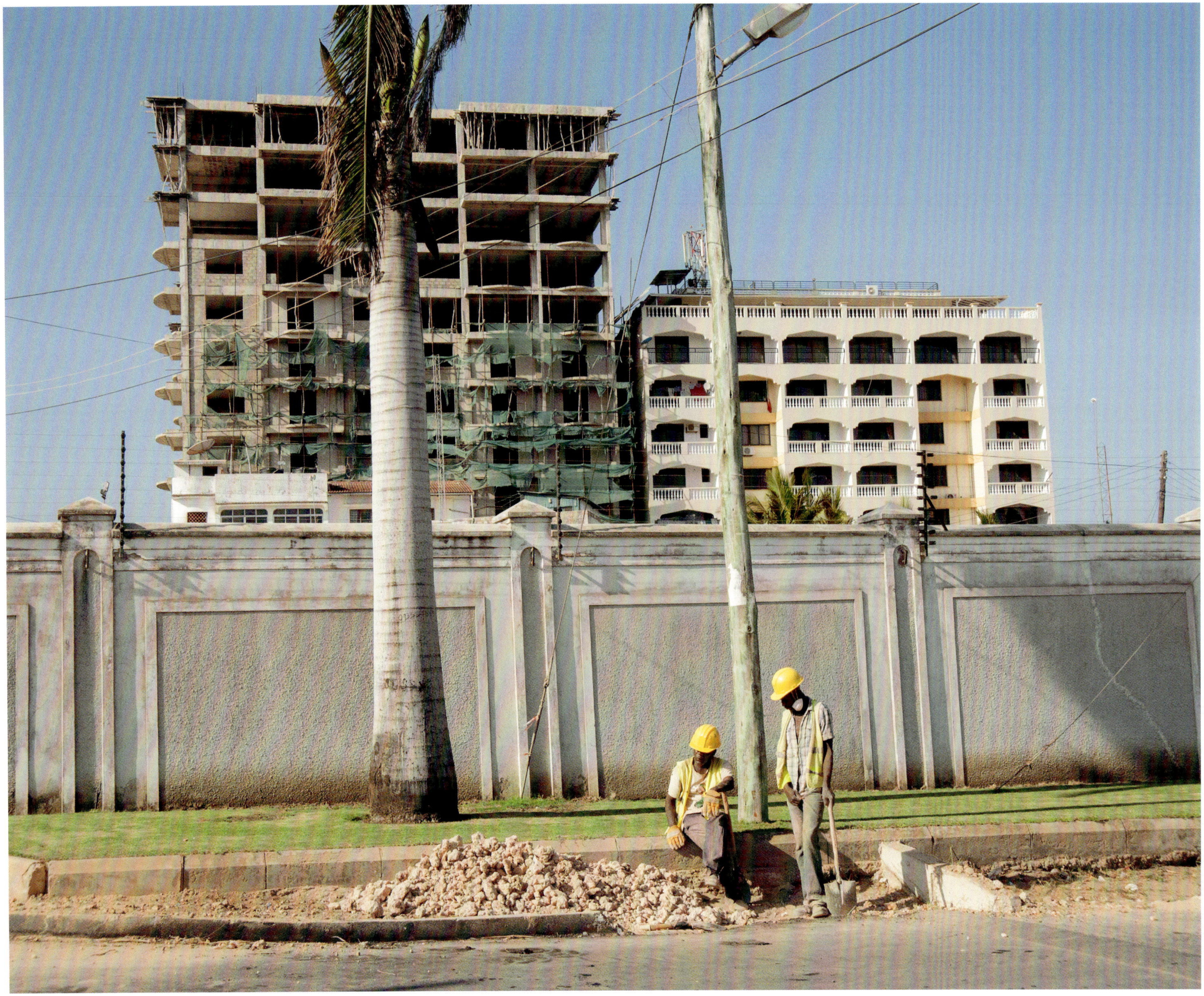

Building under construction, Mombasa Island, 2014

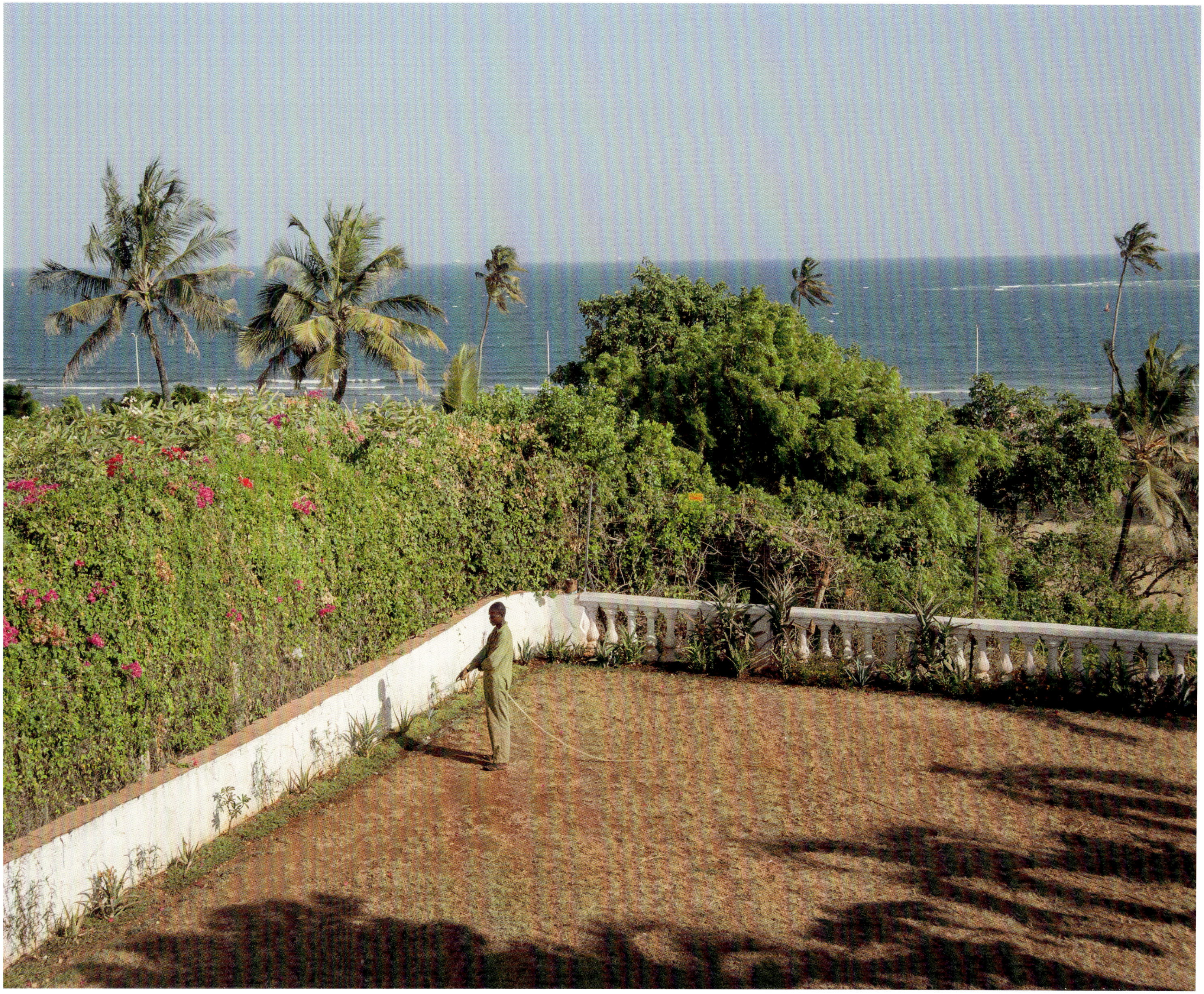

Private residence, Mombasa Island, 2014

Abandoned house, Malindi, 2013

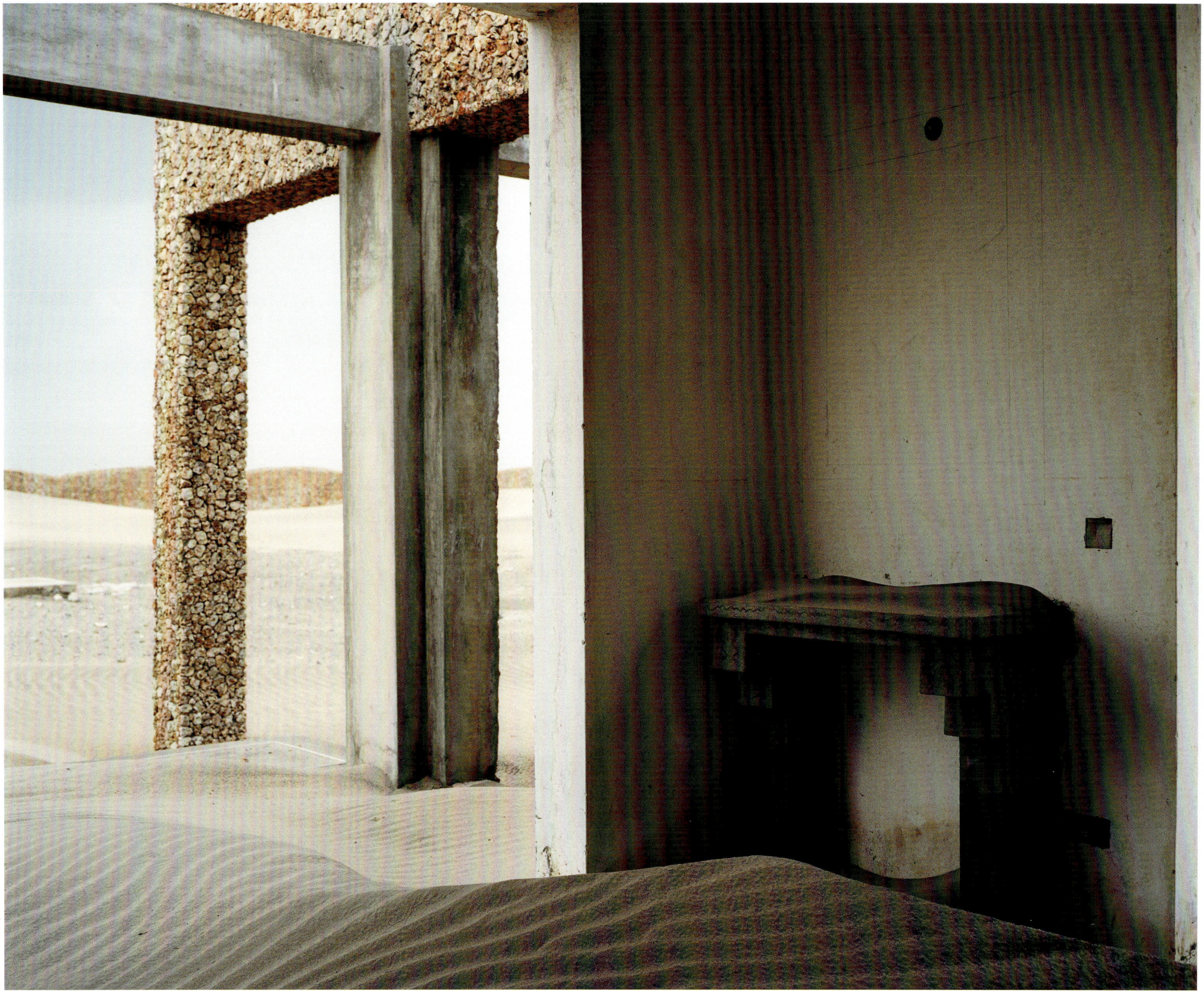

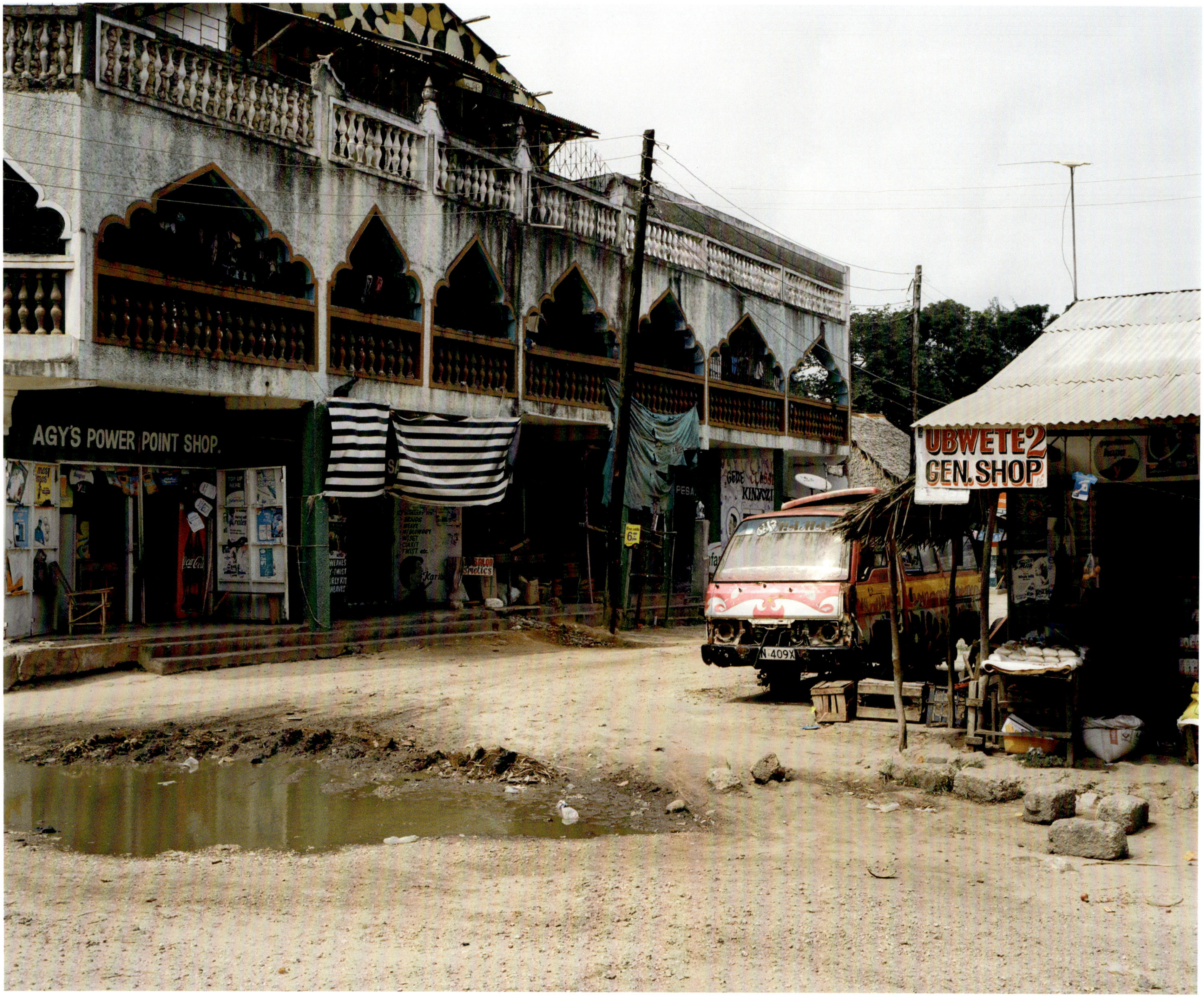

Watamu town, near Gede ruins, 2014

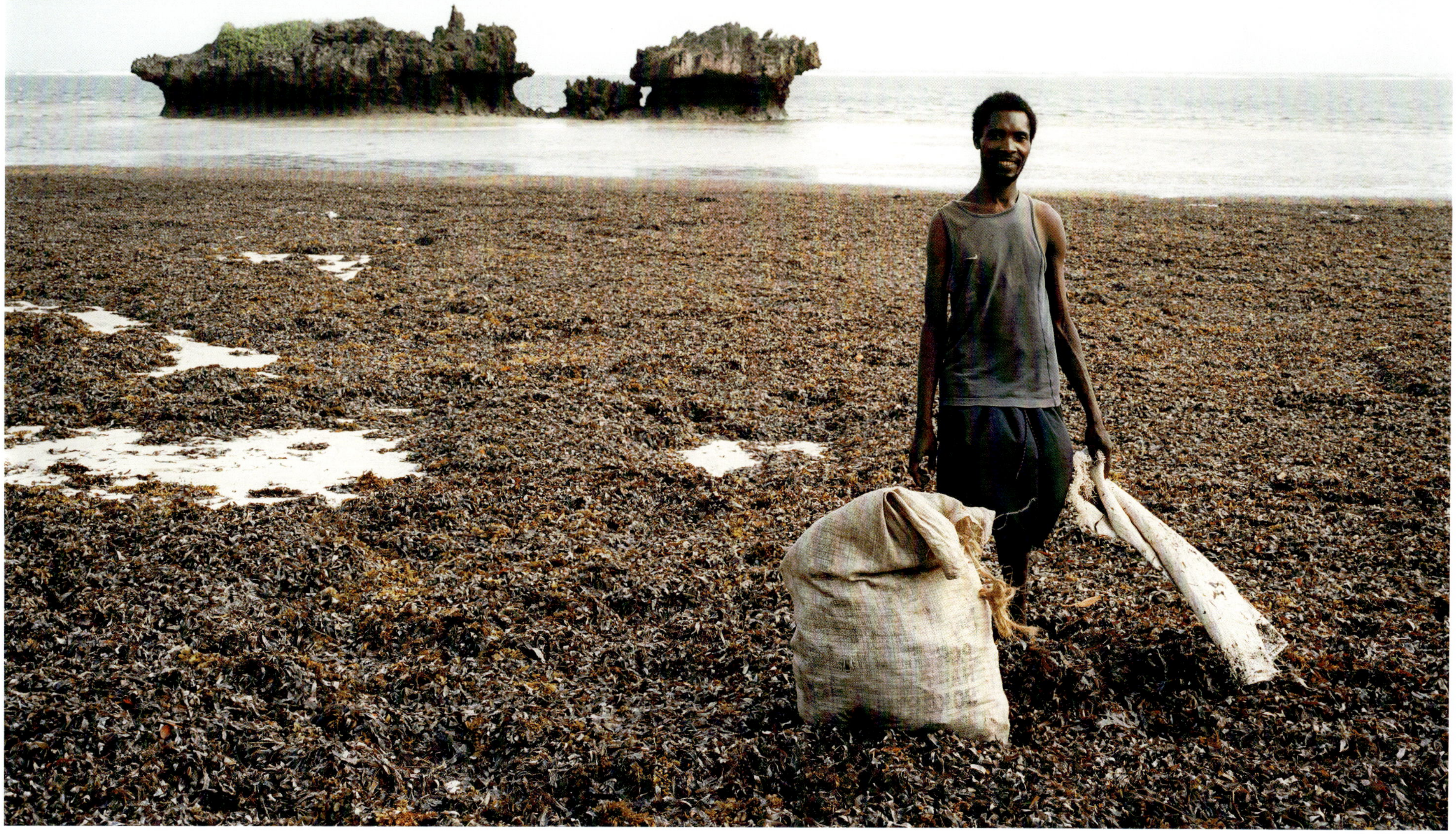

Garbage collection, Watamu, 2014

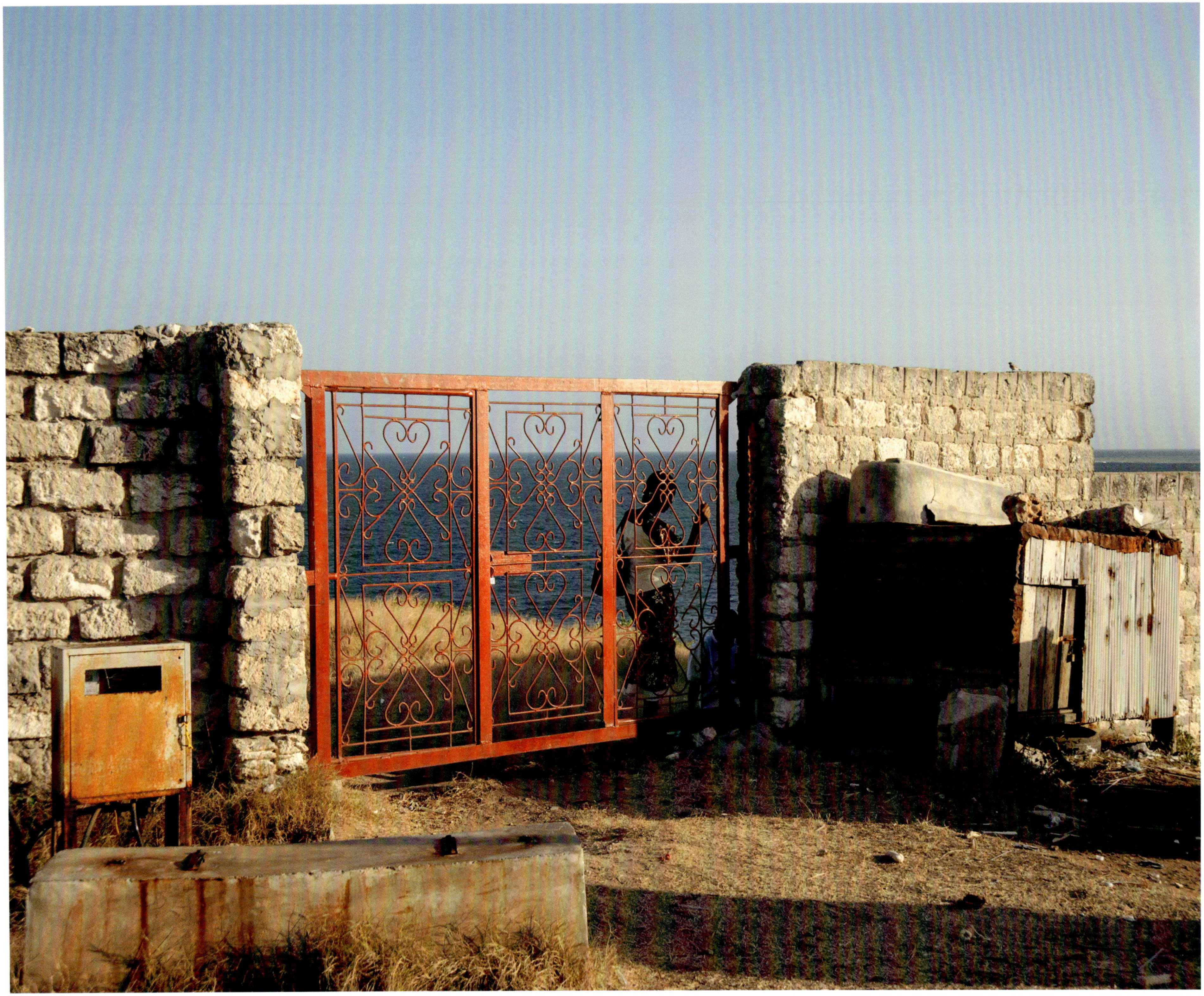

Mama Ngina Drive, Mombasa Island, 2014

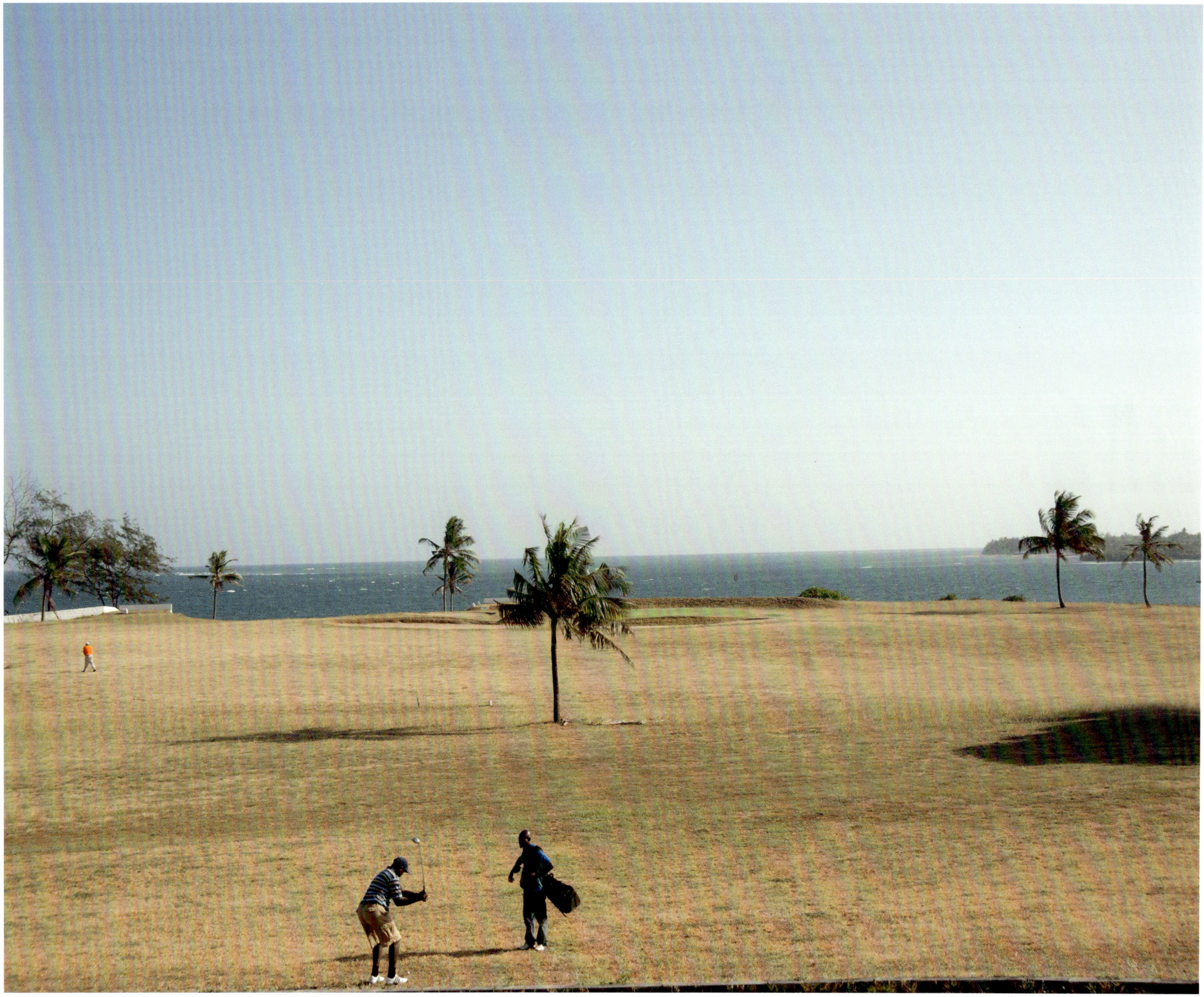

Mombasa golf club, Mombasa Island, 2014

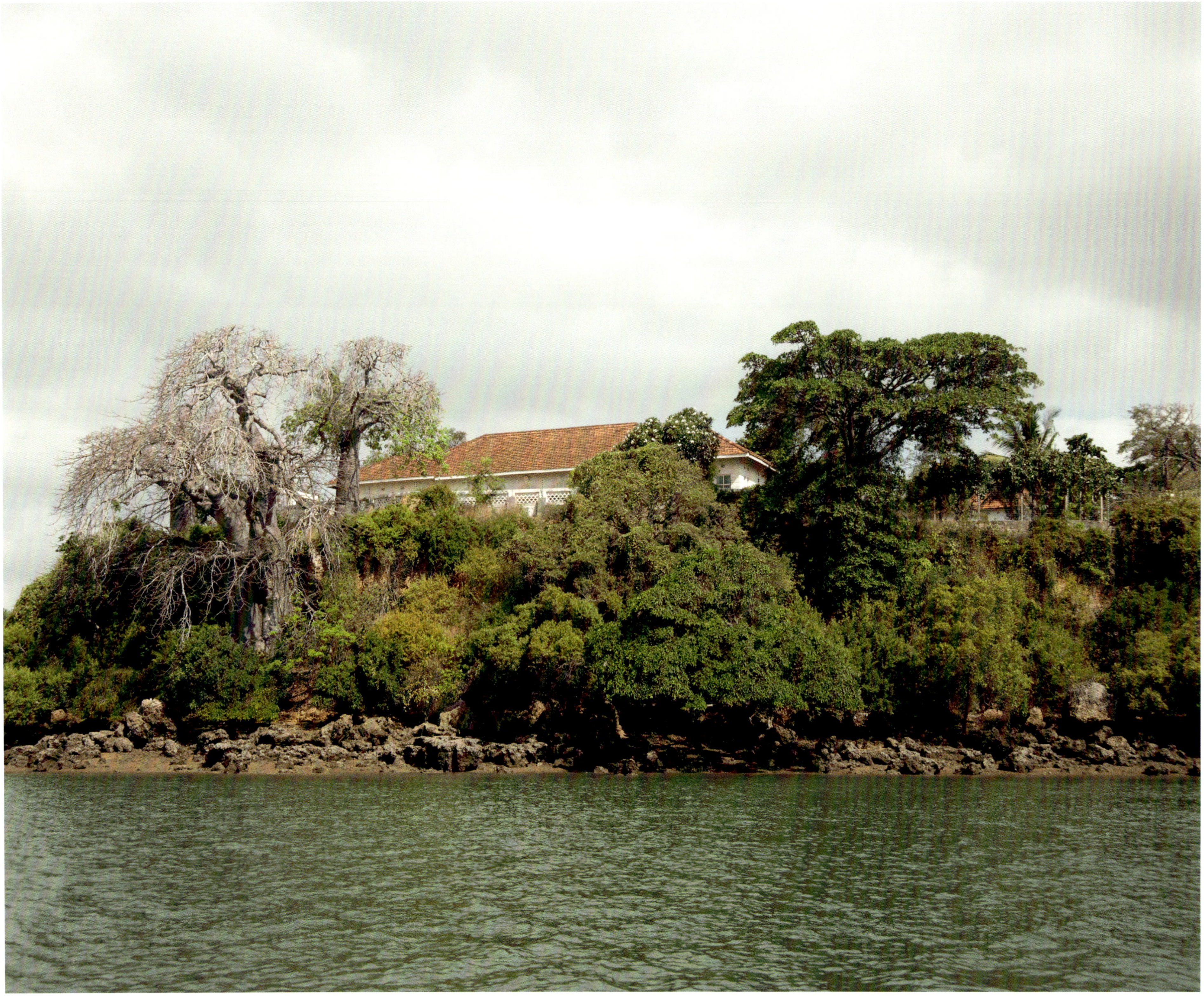

Tudor Creek, Mombasa Island, 2014

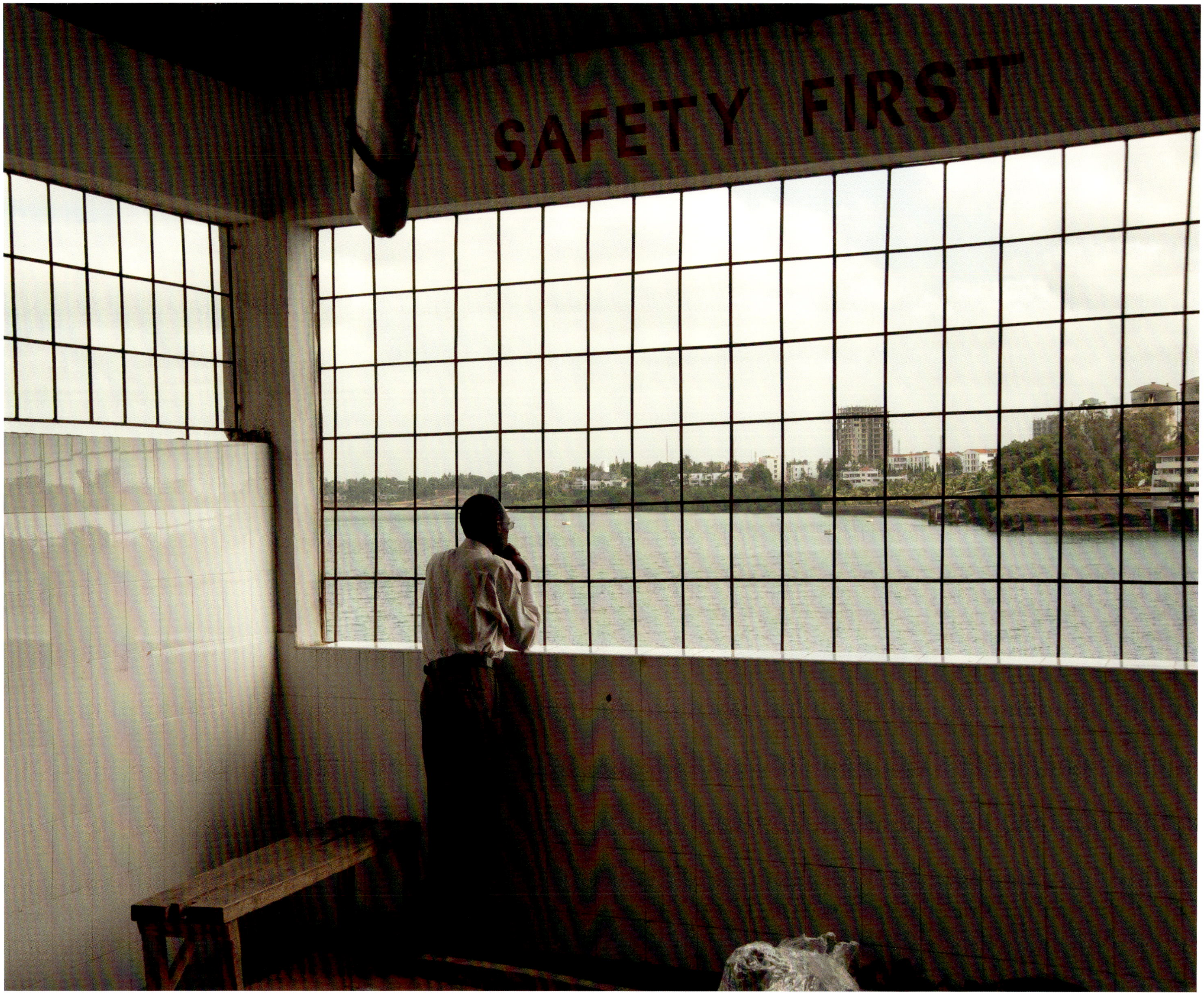

Fish market, Mombasa Island, 2014

SOMALIA

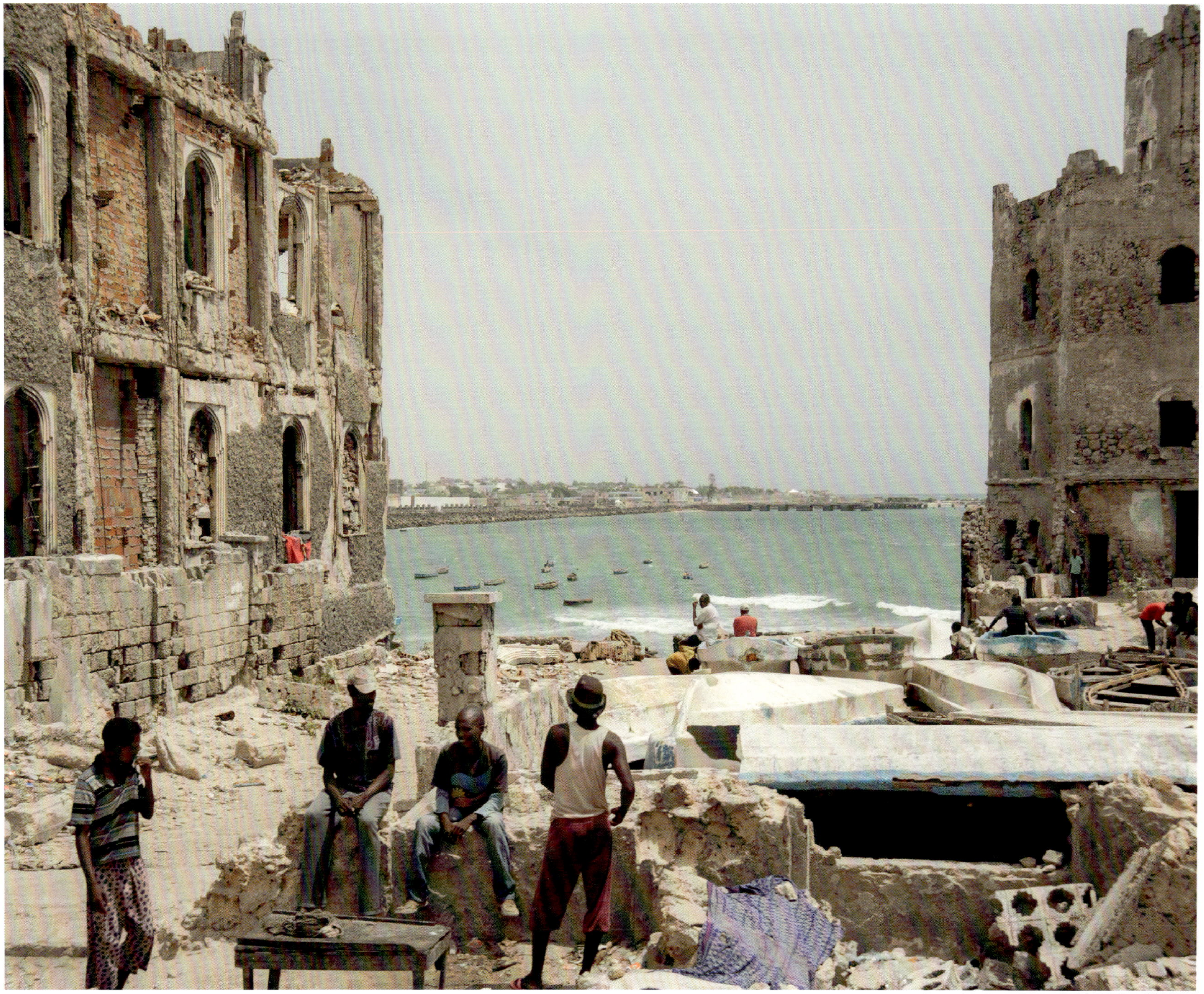

Corso Somalia near Secondo Lido beach, Mogadishu, 2013

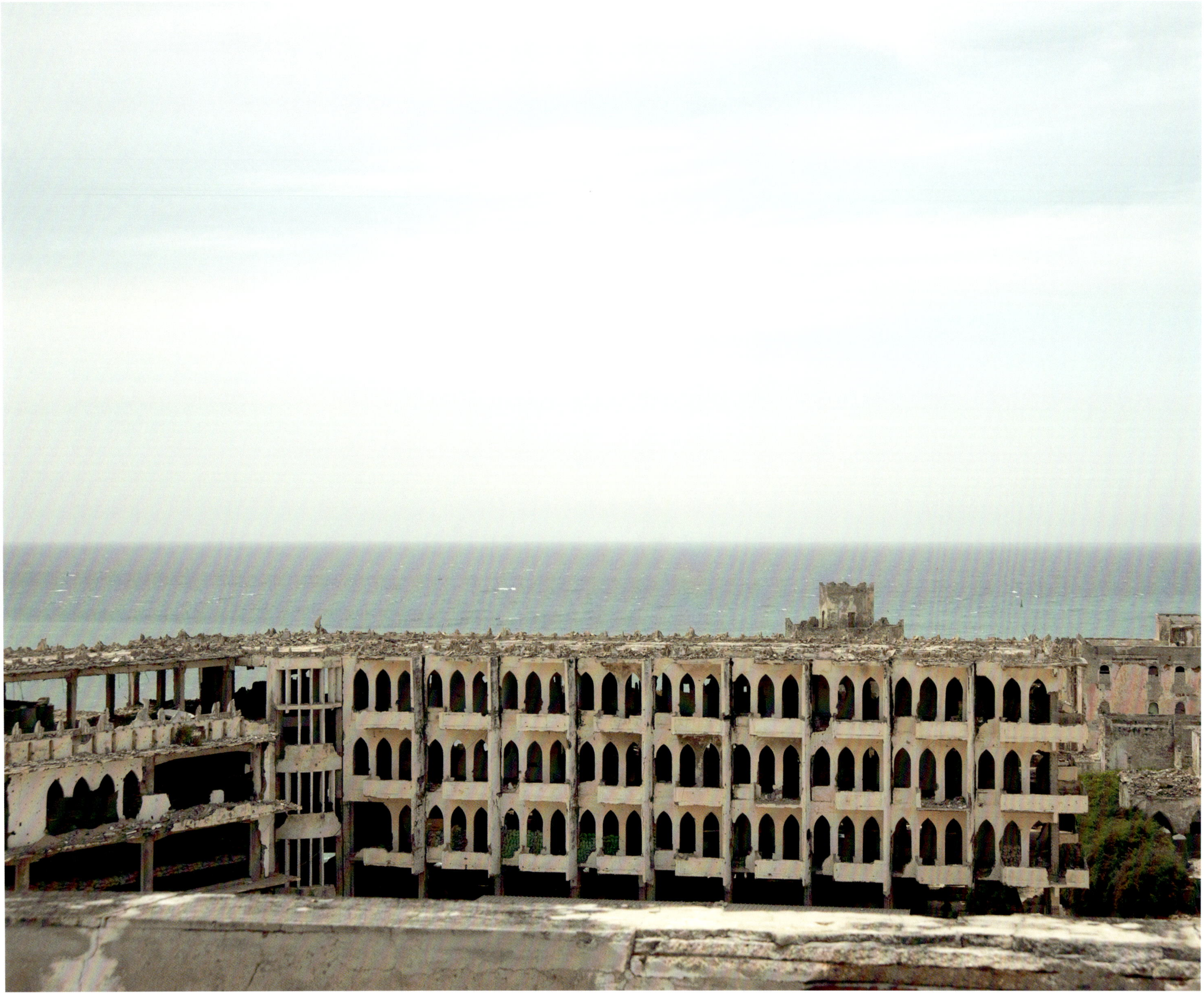

Al-Aruba Hotel, now an African Union military base, Mogadishu, 2013

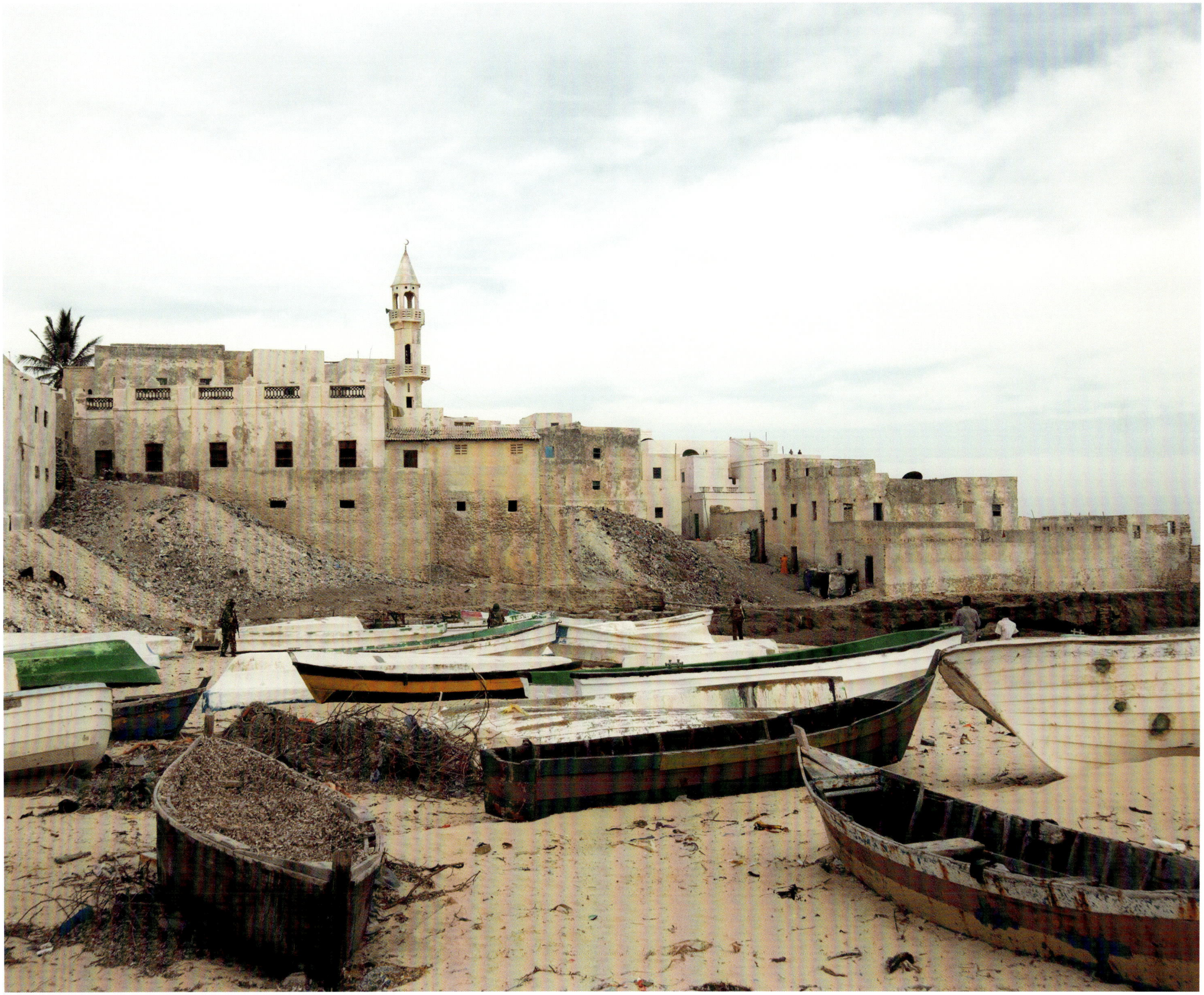

Merca seafront, 2013

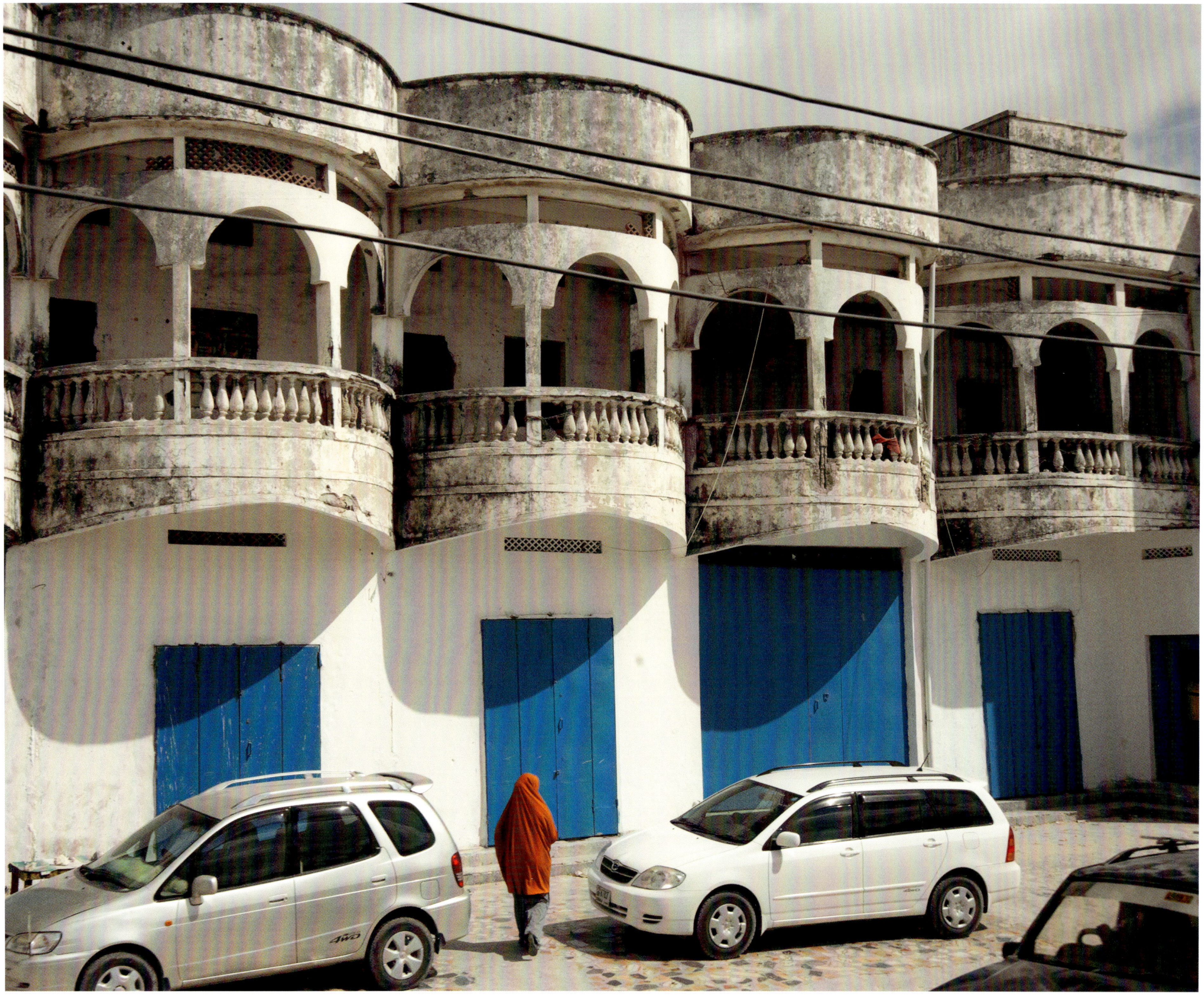

Modern building, Mogadishu, 2014

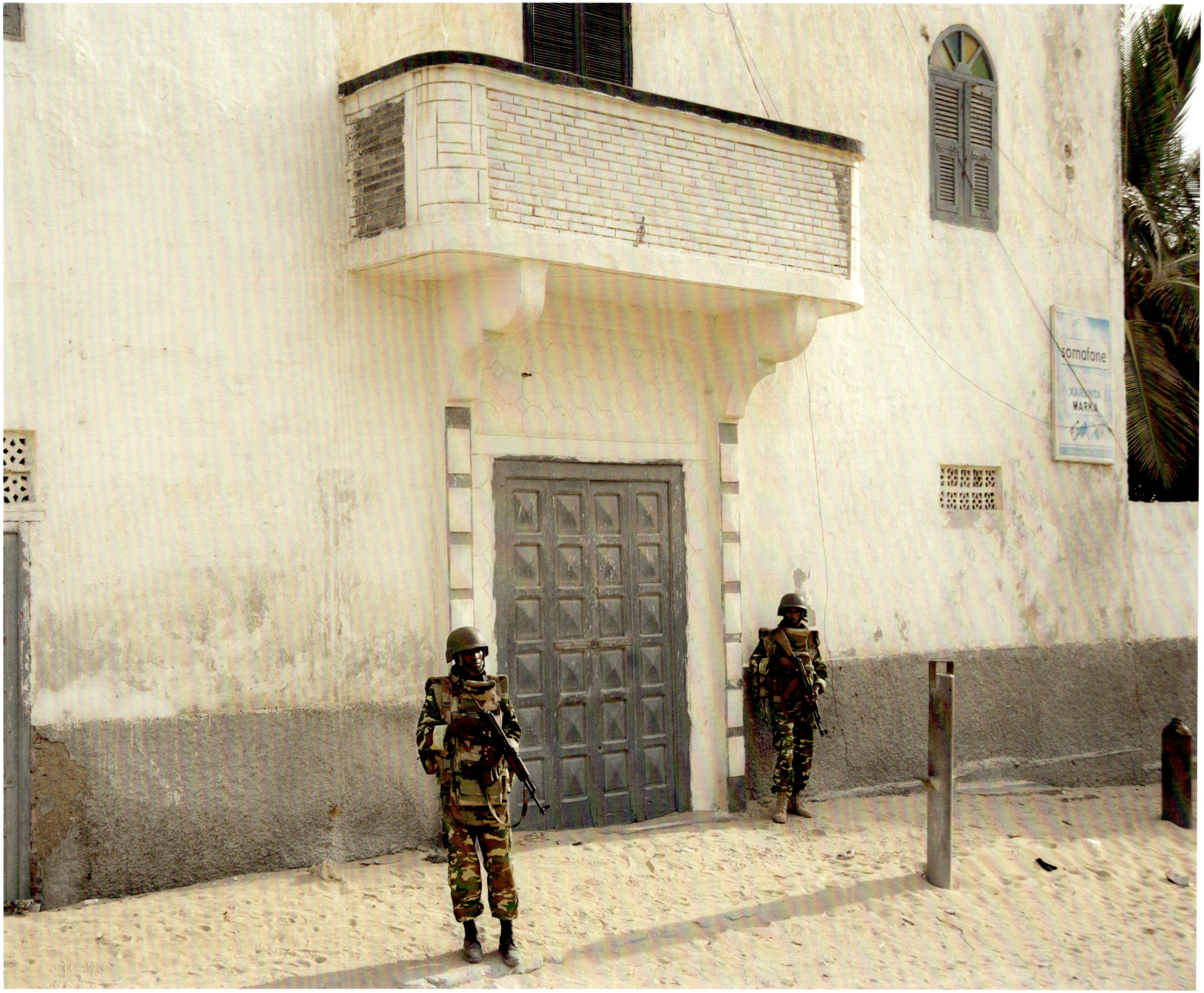

African Union forces on patrol, Merca, 2013

Mogadishu's Catholic cathedral, or what's left of it, lies along what was known as the "green line" at the beginning of the civil war. It sliced the city in two from north to south as two warlords continuously battled each other for control of "the other side." It is still a place of gunfire and violence. The first time I visited in 1993, I was with my childhood friend, the photojournalist Dan Eldon. Dan was killed not far from there a few months later. I went back in 2002. As I was walking up the cathedral steps, I suddenly heard the familiar, metallic "zinc zinc" noise of small arms fire all around me. I ran for cover behind the rubble to the right of the cathedral's entrance. The ensuing street battle scared off my hired security detail, leaving me and my translator to fend for ourselves. We were detained by the gunmen and later released. Ten years after that incident, I returned again to the cathedral. The lady in red was standing on the steps, and I quickly snapped some frames from behind the open windows of the car. When a man standing in the street saw me, the driver signaled that it was time to go. Word of my presence would spread like a bushfire, putting my life in great danger, he told me. Things hadn't changed that much.

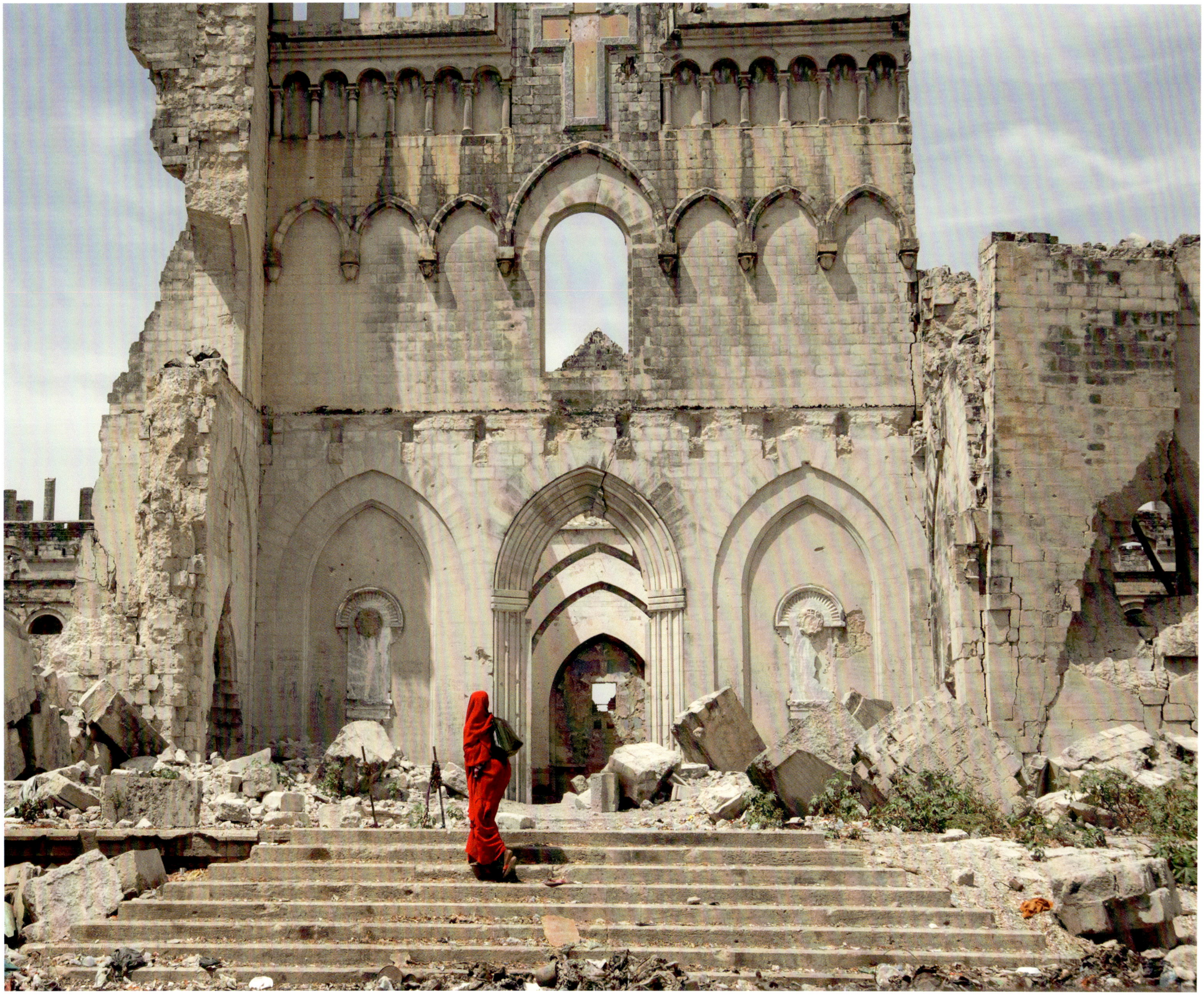

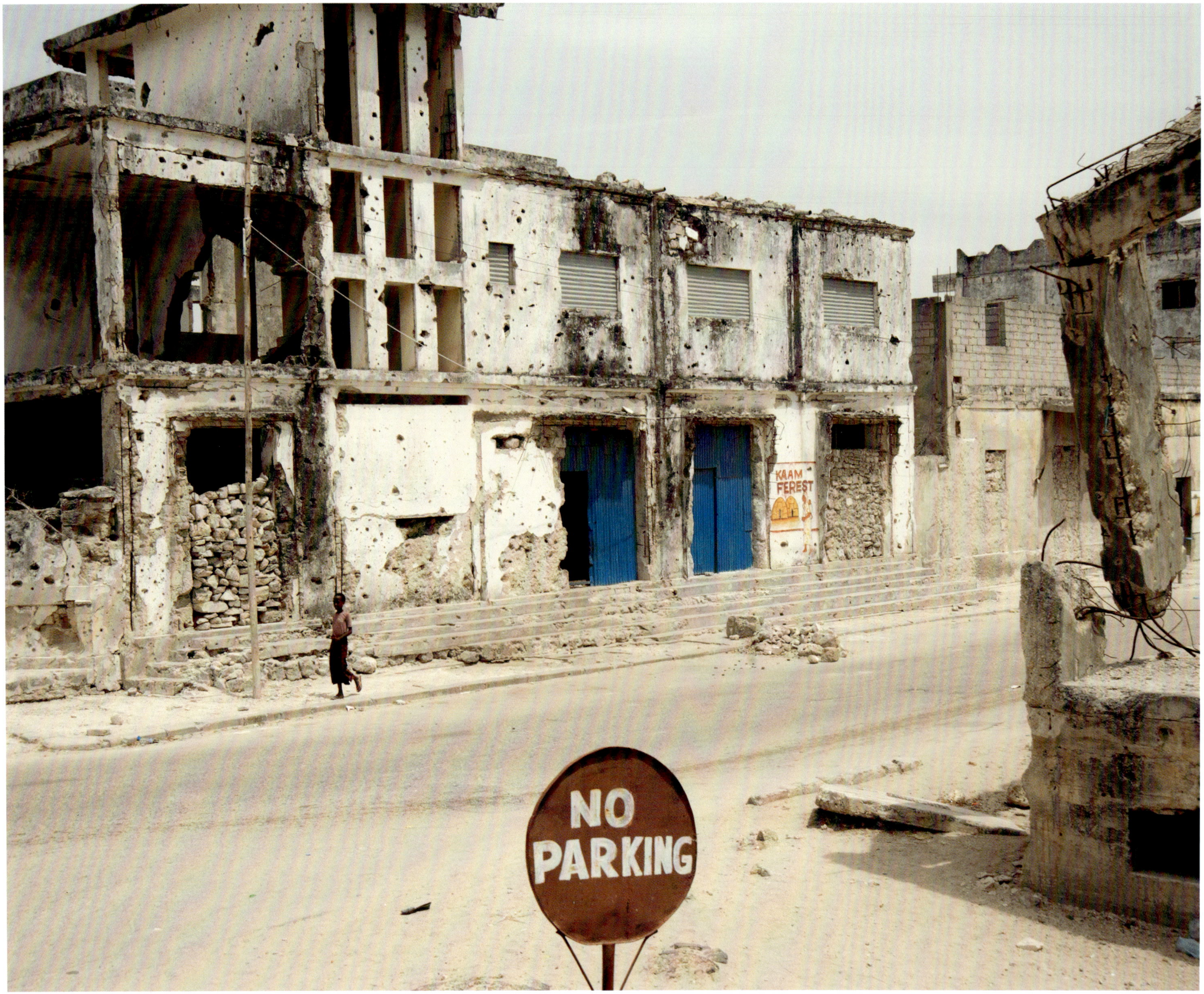

Via Ahmed Bin Idriss, Mogadishu, 2013

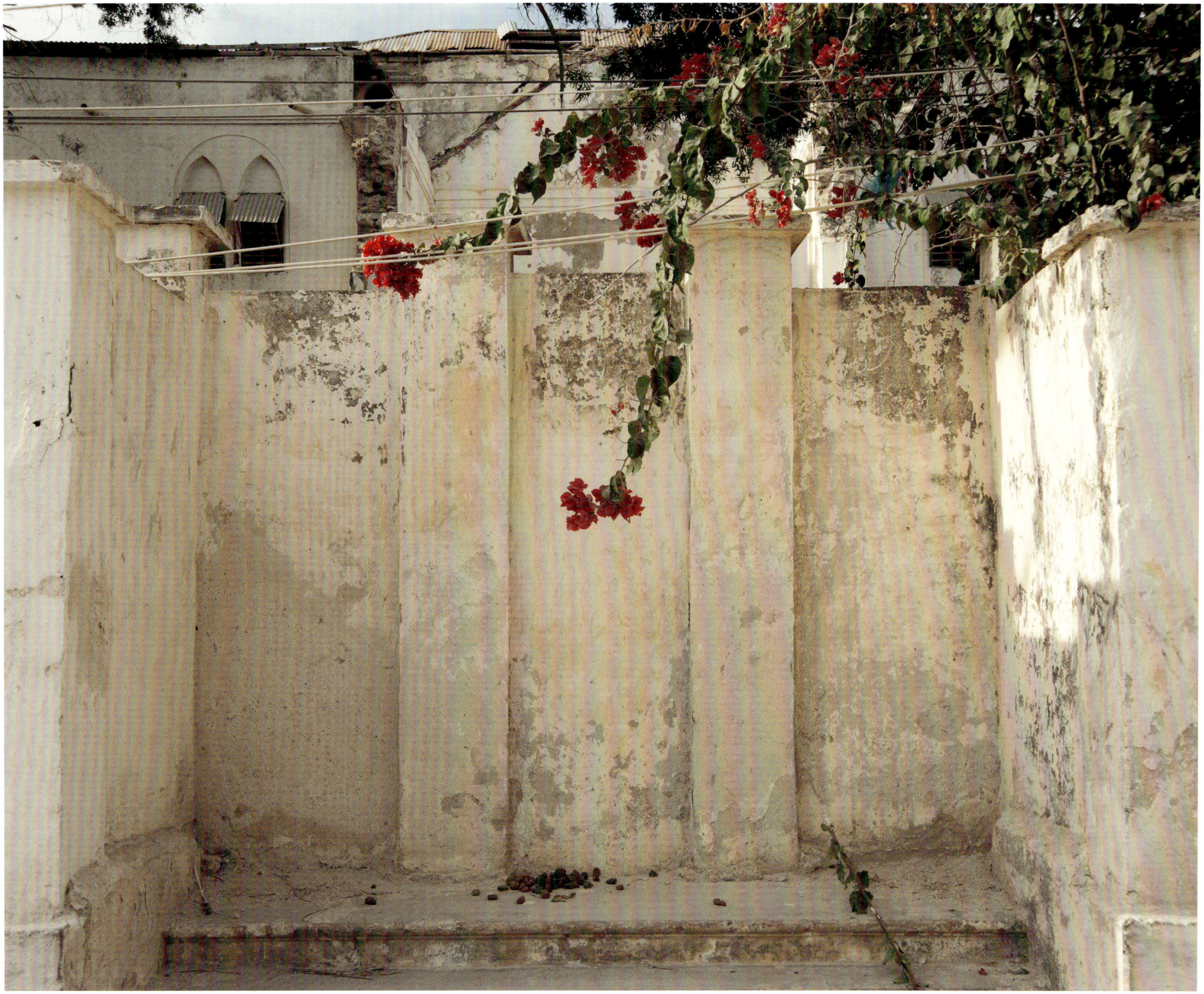

Behind the wall, an old colonial house, Merca, 2013

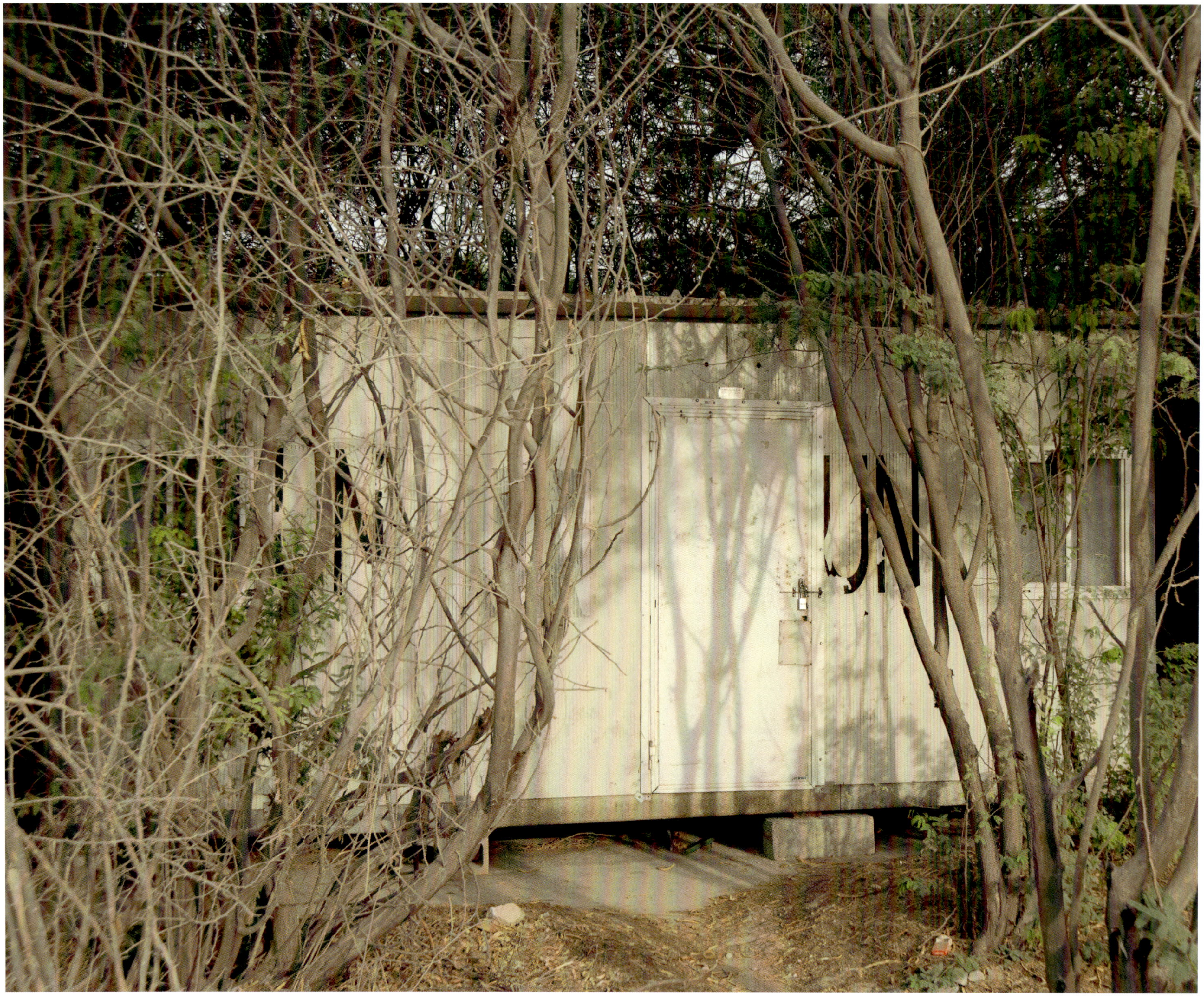

United Nations office, Mogadishu international airport, 2013

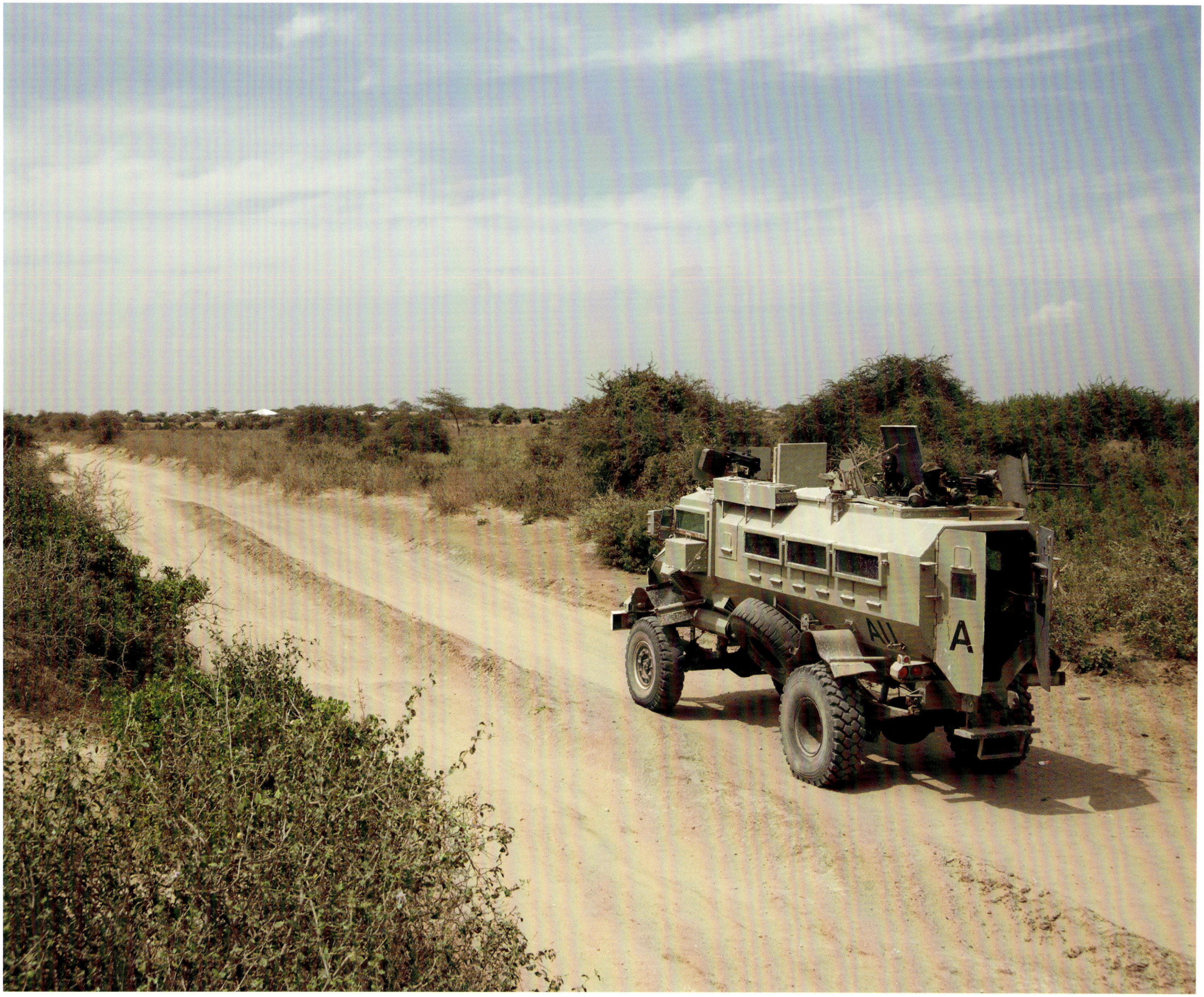

Armored personnel carrier (APC) from the African Union between Mogadishu and Merca, 2013

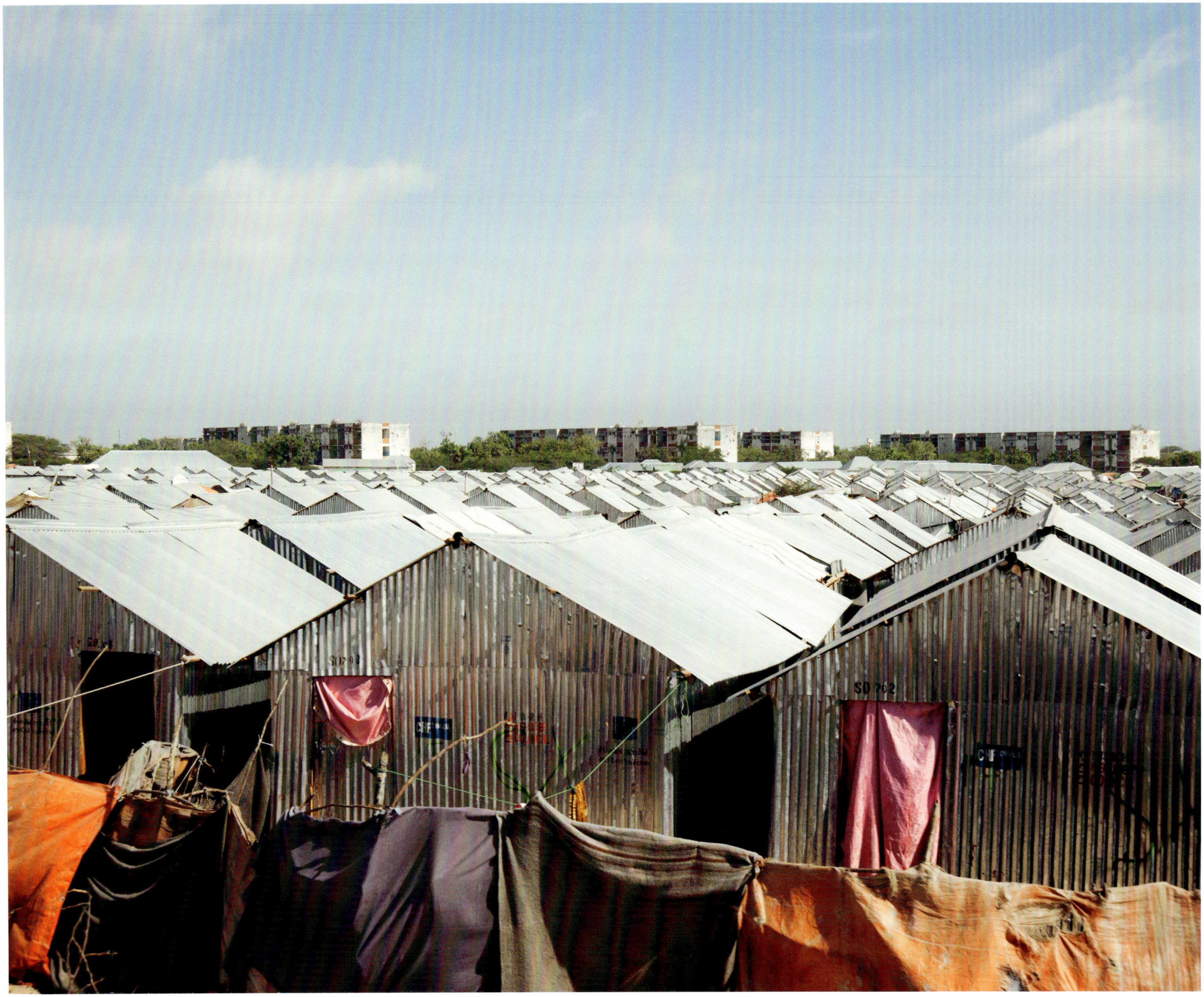

Internally displaced persons camp, Mogadishu, 2013

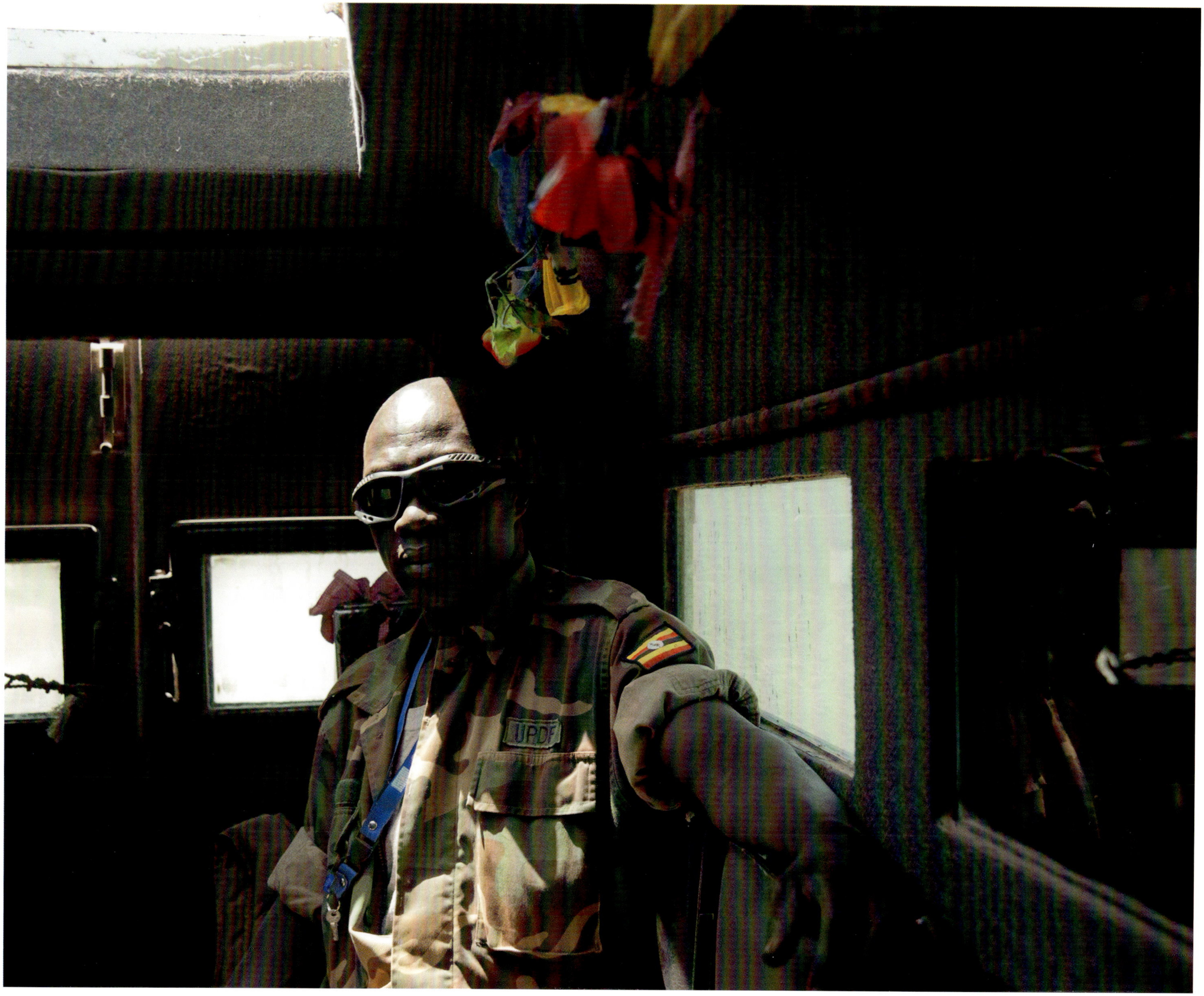

African Union soldier inside an APC military tank, Mogadishu, 2013

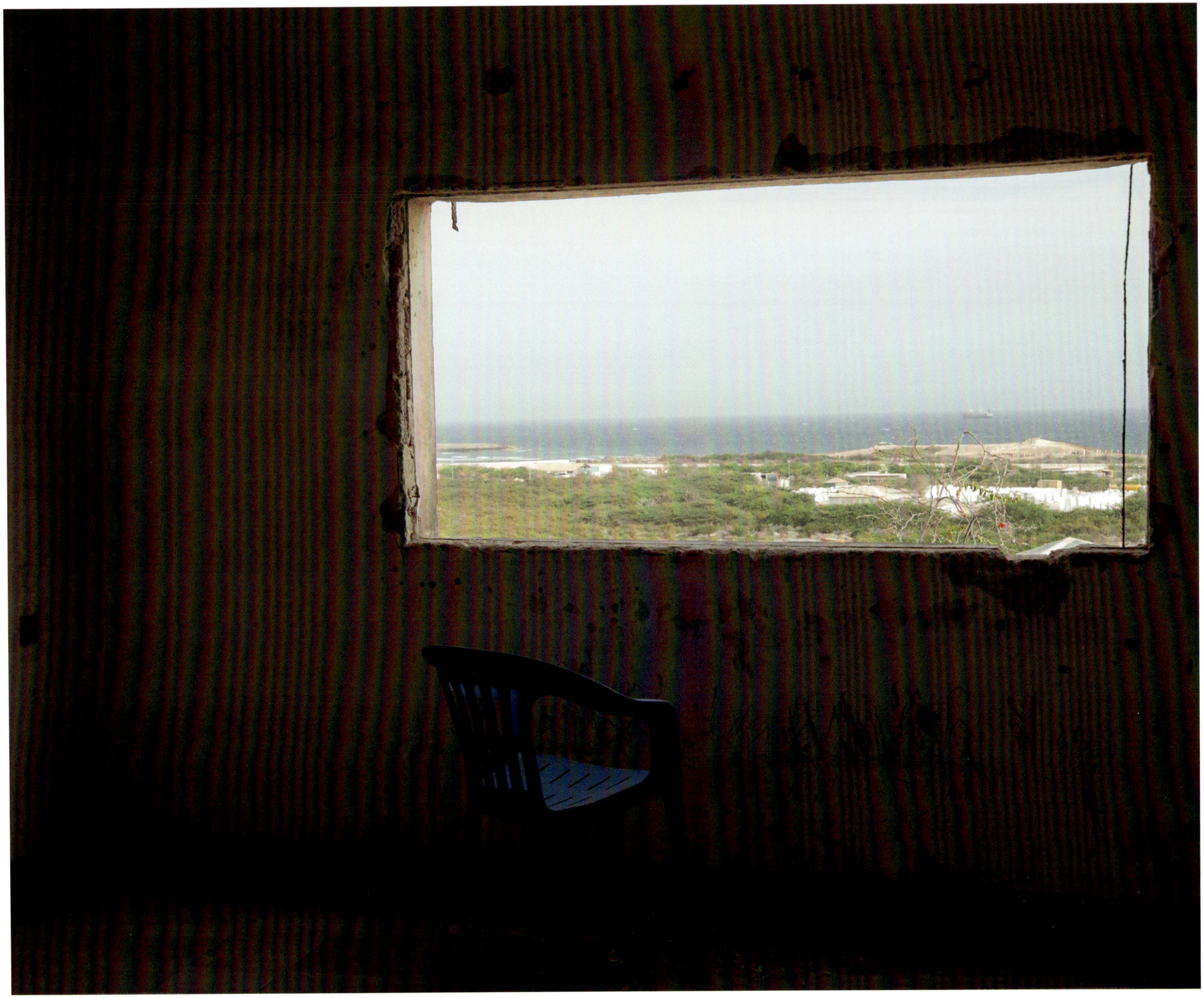

Mogadishu international airport, 2013

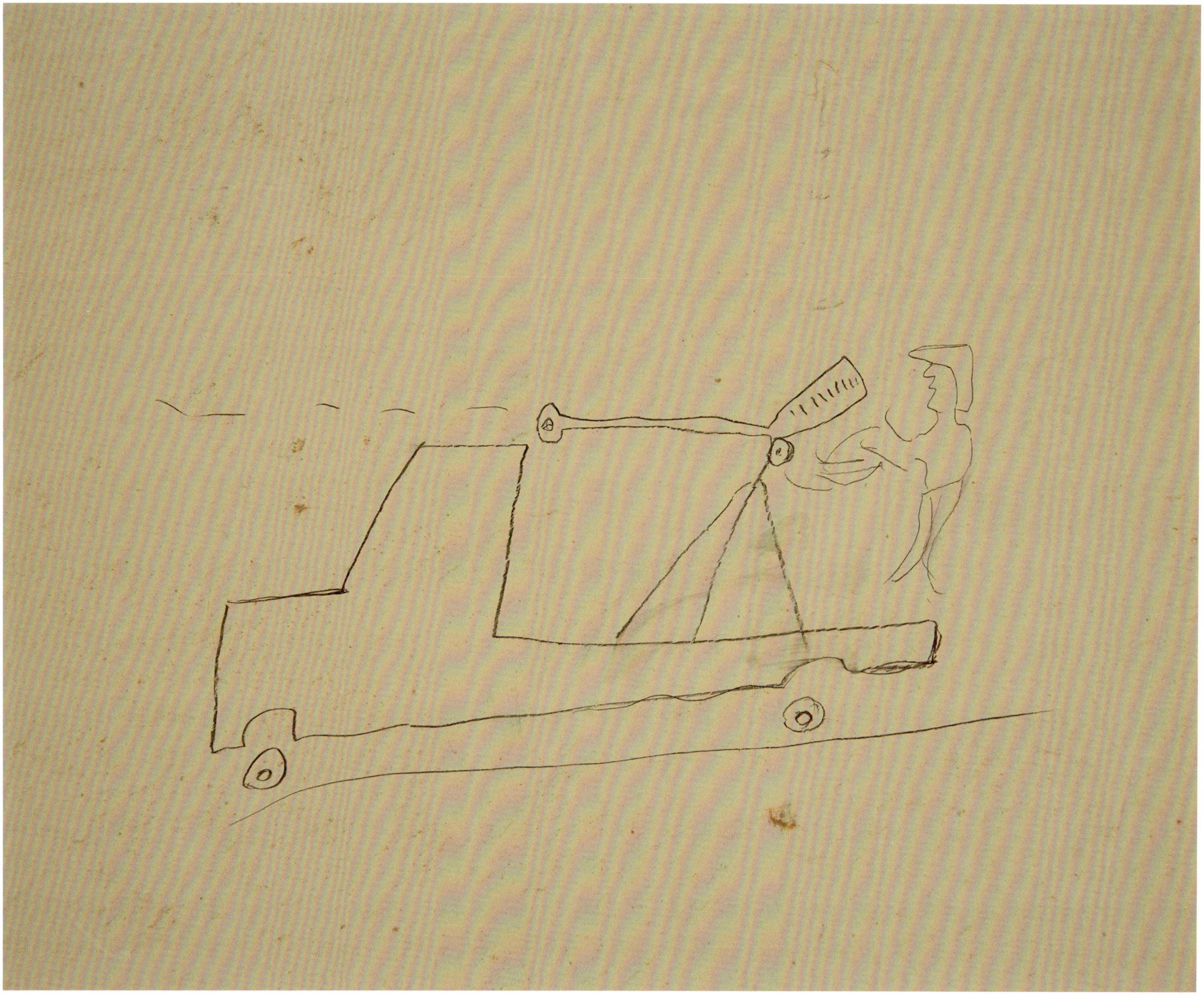

Al-Shabaab drawing, Mogadishu, 2013

View of the former business district in Mogadishu, from the former central bank building of Somalia, 2013

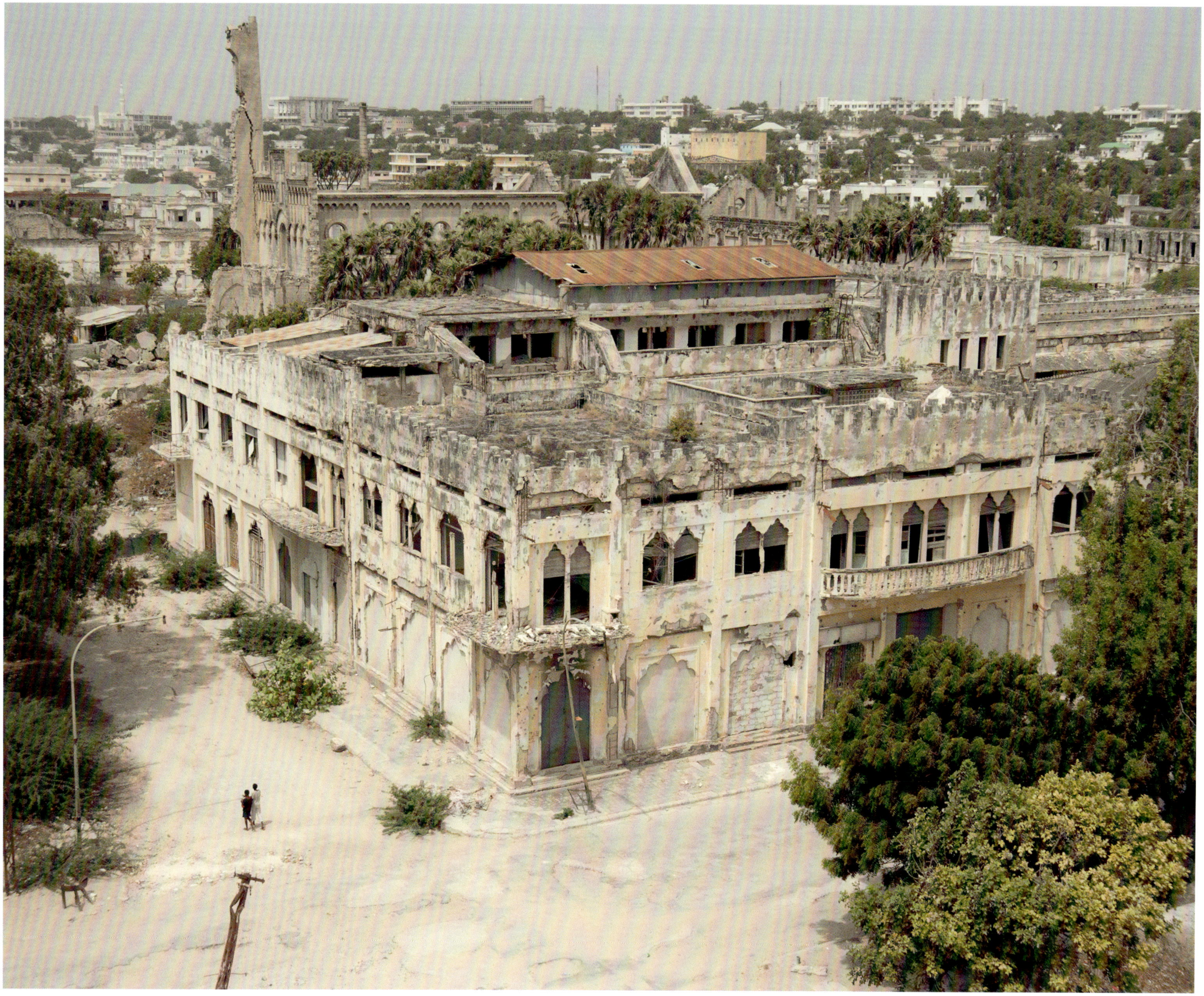

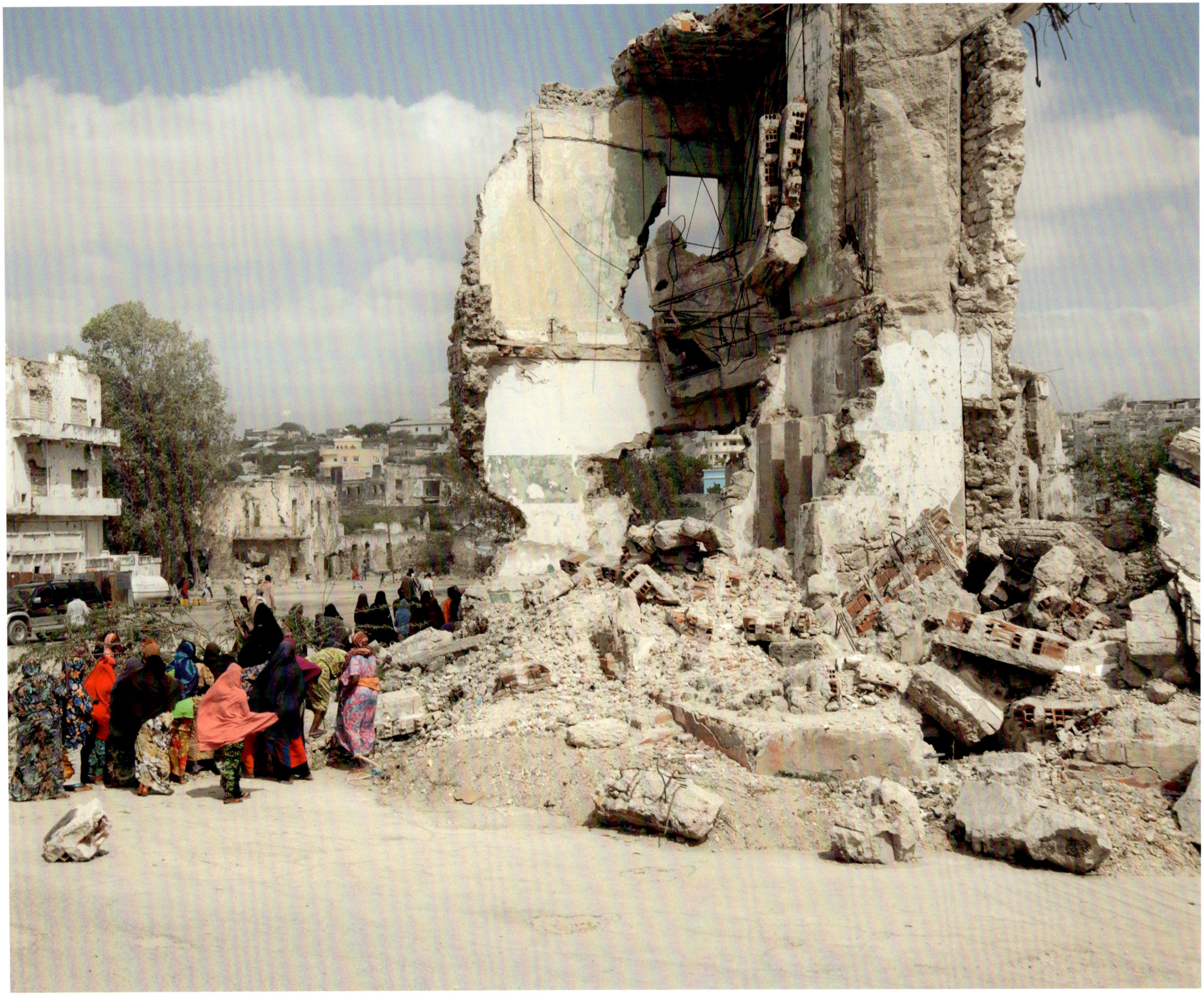

Near Mogadishu's parliament, 2013

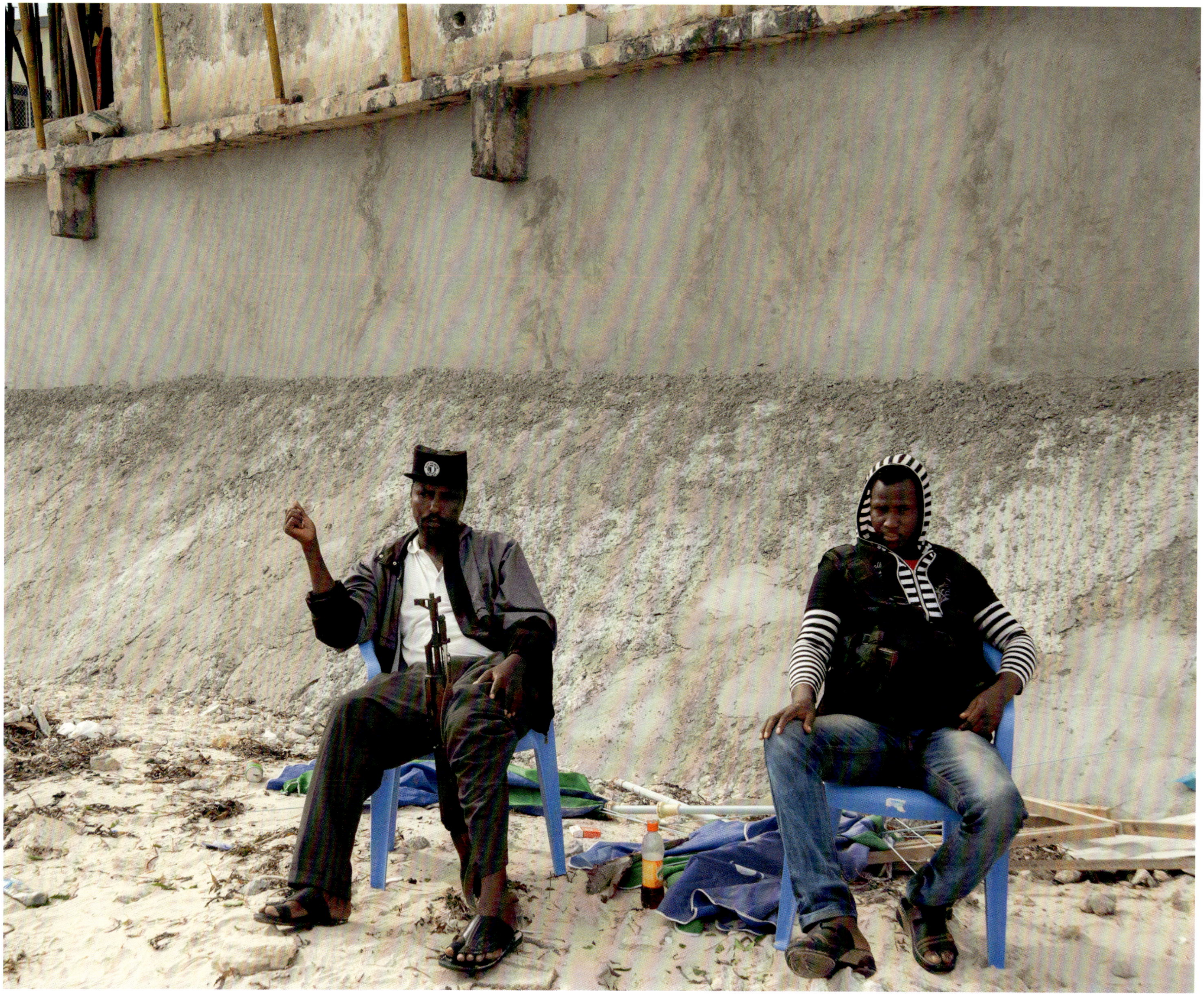

Hired gunmen providing security to nearby restaurant, Lido Beach, Mogadishu, 2013

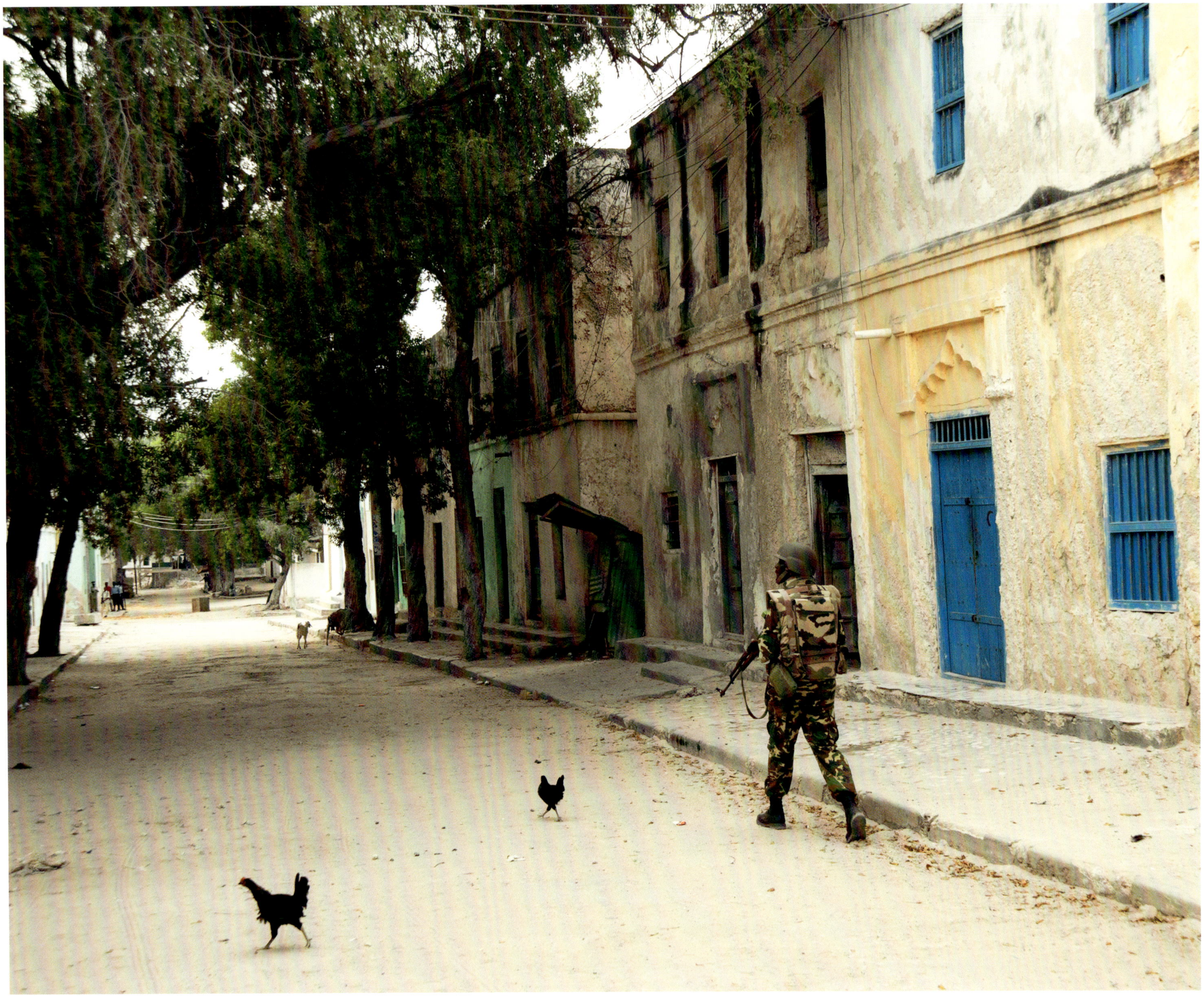

African Union forces on patrol, Merca, 2013

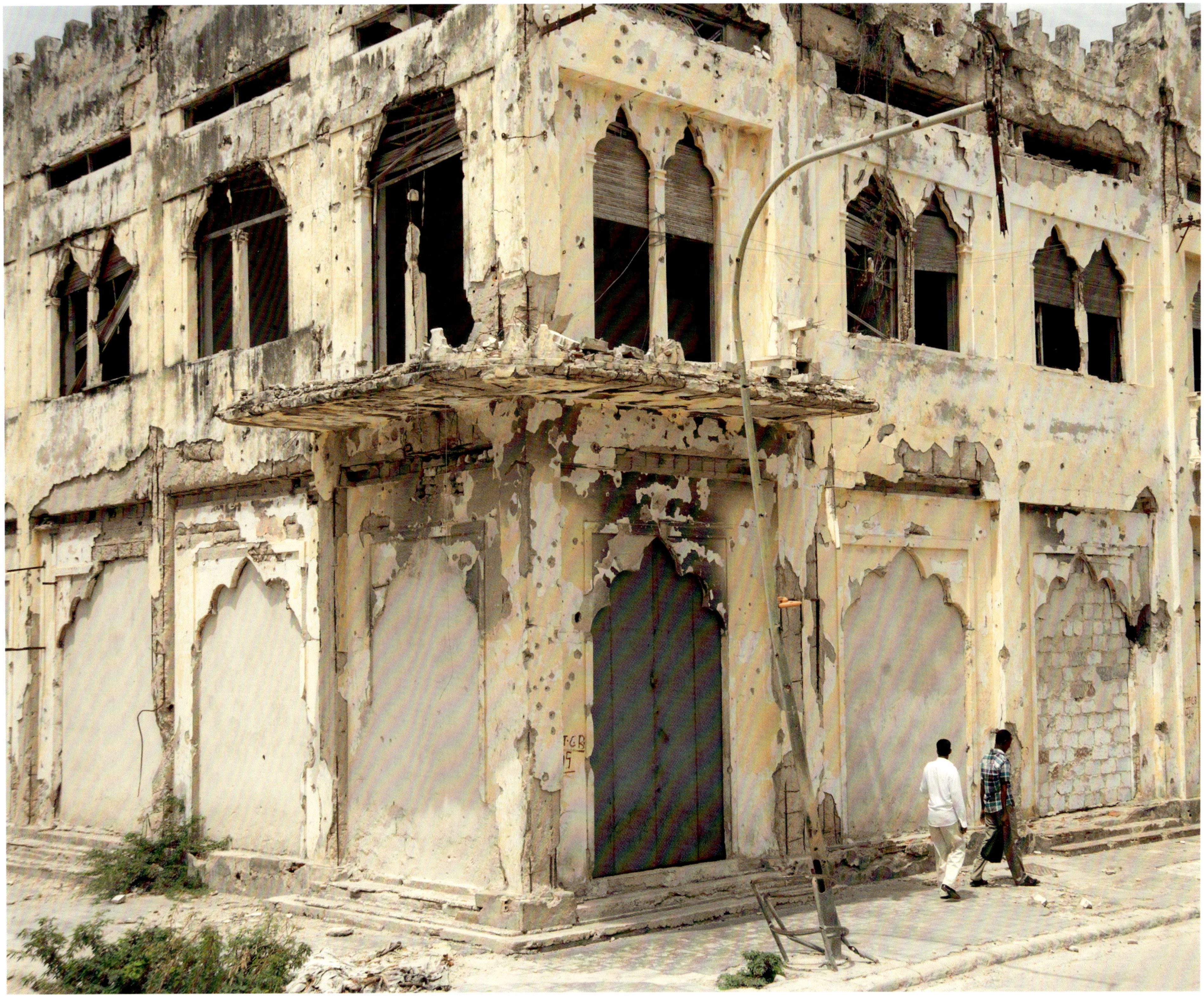

Via Corso Somalia, Mogadishu, 2013

View from the Al-Aruba hotel, now a military base for the African Union, Mogadishu, 2013

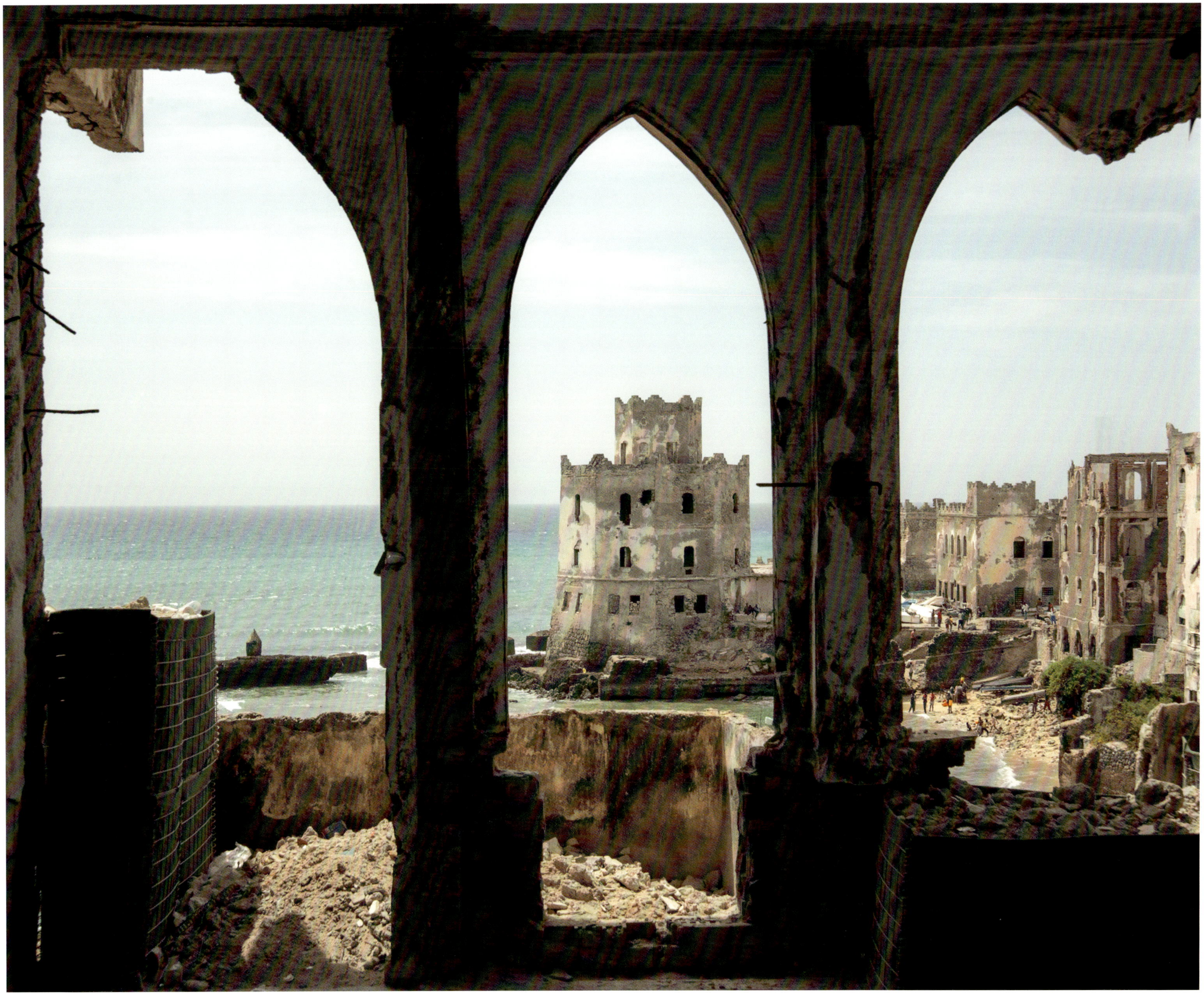

JON LEE ANDERSON

Jon Lee Anderson is an American author and journalist who began his career in the early nineteen-eighties, reporting on Central America's civil wars. As a staff writer for *The New Yorker* since 1998, he has reported from Syria, Iraq, Iran, Afghanistan, Lebanon, Somalia, Angola, Liberia, Libya, Central African Republic, Mali, South Sudan, Zimbabwe, Brazil, Cuba, Venezuela, Sri Lanka, and many other countries. Anderson has also profiled a number of international public figures, including Gabriel Garcia Márquez, Augusto Pinochet, Fidel Castro, Hugo Chávez, Mahmoud Ahmadinejad, and King Juan Carlos.

Anderson is also the author of a biography on the iconic Marxist revolutionary Ernesto Che Guevara. Entitled *Che Guevara: A Revolutionary Life,* it was first published in 1997. While researching the book in Bolivia, he discovered the hidden location of Guevara's skeletal remains, after which they were exhumed and returned to Cuba. Anderson has written several other books, including *Guerrillas: Journeys in the Insurgent World, The Lion's Grave: Dispatches from Afghanistan,* and *The Fall of Baghdad*. Anderson is currently writing his next book, a biography of Fidel Castro.

GUILLAUME BONN

Guillaume Bonn is third generation of a French family all born in Madagascar. He studied Economics and International Politics at Université de Montréal and Université du Québec à Montréal and graduated from the International Center of Photography in New York. For the last twenty years, he has reported on conflict, social and environment issues. He and writer Marc Lacey were the first journalists to cover the Darfur crisis from inside Sudan for *The New York Times* and uncovered the sexual abuse committed against children in Congo by United Nations peacekeepers. Bonn is the recipient of several awards and author of three photographic books, including his first monograph, *Le Mal d'Afrique: A Journey into Old and New Africa*.

He has directed a number of documentaries, including *Peter Beard: Scrapbooks from Africa and Beyond* on the American artist, which was screened at the Sundance Film Festival and shown on TV channels worldwide. Bonn also worked as a cameraman on *Dying to Tell the Story,* a ninety-minute *CNN* documentary nominated for an Emmy Award. He is a contributor to *Vanity Fair* magazine, covering a range of stories, including the conflict in North Uganda with the late Christopher Hitchens, the murder of conservationist Joan Root near Lake Naivasha, and "Agony and Ivory" on African elephants and the ivory trade. Bonn is also a visual contributor to everydayafrica and Memo Paris and is a board member of the African Network for Animal Welfare (ANAW).

ACKNOWLEDGMENTS

Without the help of RAK, Clara and John Molloy this book would never have seen the light of day—thank you!

My deepest thanks to Mary Anne Fitzgerald for her constant support in the preparation of this project and for making her home a welcoming haven. To Yves Bonn and Anigue Malignon for being there and keeping an eye on me.

SPECIAL THANKS

Amy Harmon
Andre Laget
Susan White
James Crump
Ron Beinner
Pierre Zanger
Laurent Hutin
Nigel Archer
Alex Polier
Sabine Heller
Pierre Burton
Sibylle Luig
Amanda Ross
Austin Peck
Laila Said
Daniela Agneli
Peter Silvester
Julia Wagner
Carolyn Roumeguere
Isabelle Roumeguere
Yaron Schwartzman
Wendell Steavenson
Jean-Claude Luyat
Michelle Anderson
Ambroise Tezenas
Tara Fitzgerald
Petra Fitzgerald
Jennifer Pastore
Philippe Gourdin
Daire O'Reilly
Neil McCarthy
Graydon Carter
Suzanne Said
Myriam Said
Julianna Stobbs
Karen Howes

~ To MEMO PARIS for their support ~
~ Dan Eldon for being a constant inspiration ~
~ Jon Lee Anderson for his wonderful foreword ~

COLOPHON

Mosquito Coast by Guillaume Bonn
Foreword by Jon Lee Anderson

Design:
Julia Wagner, grafikanstalt
Guillaume Bonn

Copyediting:
Dawn Michelle d'Atri

Project management:
Cassandra Edlefsen Lasch, Hatje Cantz

Production:
Julia Günther, Hatje Cantz

Reproductions:
Laurent Hutin, Janvier, Paris

Printing:
Offsetdruckerei Karl Grammlich GmbH, Pliezhausen

Typeface:
Alright sans, Tiempos

Paper:
BVS matt, 170 g/m²

Binding:
Lachenmaier GmbH, Reutlingen

Published by
Hatje Cantz Verlag
Zeppelinstrasse 32
73760 Ostfildern
Germany
Tel. +49 711 4405-200
Fax +49 711 4405-220
www.hatjecantz.com
A Ganske Publishing Group company

Hatje Cantz books are available internationally at selected bookstores. For more information about our distribution partners, please visit our website at www.hatjecantz.com.

ISBN 978-3-7757-3968-9

Printed in Germany

Cover illustration:
Cathedral of Mogadishu, 2013

MEMO
PARIS